Haunted Wisconsin

HAUNTED WISCONSIN

Beth Scott   &   Michael Norman

HEARTLANDPRESS
an imprint of NorthWord inc.

*To Larry and Janell, without whose
patience and understanding this book
would not have been possible.*

First Printing, October 1980
Second Printing, July 1982
Third Printing, June 1984
Fourth Printing, March 1986
Fifth Printing, October 1987
Sixth Printing, November 1988

  Heartland Press
  NorthWord Press Inc.
  Box 1360
  Minocqua, WI 54548

Library of Congress Cataloging in Publication Data
Scott, Beth, 1922–
    Haunted Wisconsin.
    Bibliography: p.
    1. Ghosts–Wisconsin.   2. Legends–Wisconsin.
I. Norman, Michael, 1947–   joint author. II.   Title.
BF1472.U6S37   133.1'09775   80-22151
ISBN 0-942802-78-0

Book Design by Marian Lefebvre.
Printed in the United States of America

Contents

Preface

Nobody knows when, where, or why the first ghost walked this earth. But from the time that earliest man gathered around a circle of fire, words were whispered about unreal presences in the night . . . shadows of the dead which refused to die. The stories were passed down through the ages, from culture to culture, and eventually adapted and elaborated upon until mankind grew increasingly fearful of "seeing a ghost." We remain fascinated by the possibility of encountering these things that defy scientific explanation.

Are there *really* such things as ghosts? Our rational minds tell us that "ghost stories" are just that—fiction created to scare little boys and girls and the faint-hearted. We can accept computers, space travel, holography, and molecular photographs much more readily than "things that go bump in the night." Cynics place ghost stories in the category of UFOs, Big Foot, and the Loch Ness Monster and scorn anyone reporting an encounter with any of them. How then can we explain studies that indicate that over one half of the people surveyed believe in UFOs and some of the other "monsters"? Although we haven't seen any similar studies about belief in ghosts, we would venture to say that results might be the same!

Literally thousands of people in every nation of the world have reported encounters with ghosts. What is it they have seen?

The most accepted definition of a ghost is that it is a disembodied spirit, usually of a dead person, which haunts a person or former habitat. All ghosts are not the same. G.N.M. Tyrrell, in his classic British study, *Apparitions,* says ghosts are of four distinct types:

(1) a "crisis apparition" that occurs when a living person sees, hears, or feels the presence of another person who is experiencing a serious difficulty; (2) an apparition that occurs when a living person has tried deliberately to place his image before another person in a distant place; (3) one that appears long after the person represented by the vision has died; and (4) one that appears in a certain house, or other locale, often giving it the reputation of being "haunted."

If we are to accept the *possibility* of ghosts, how can they be explained? Parapsychologists attribute this psychic phenomenon to one of two explanations: (1) the ghost is the actual spirit of a dead person, and the person experiencing the haunting has no role in creating the vision; (2) the ghost is produced primarily by the human being experiencing the apparition. The latter view is much more widely held by scientists investigating psychic happenings. Just as television pictures are transmitted through radio waves, so a person may be able to transmit a telepathic image through space to a receiver. The picture is then reconstructed by the human being receiving the mental image. Tyrrell's crisis apparition ghost would fit this explanation, as would cases of telepathic transmittal of images between individuals.

But what of ghosts that appear long after death? The psyche (or spirit or mind) of a person may be able to survive physical death, researchers say. The body and psyche separate after death. The spirit may then survive in a different dimension with the capability of manifesting itself in a pseudo-physical form. This would partially explain why ghosts are often transparent, leave no footprints, and are unencumbered by the laws of nature, e.g., being able to move through solid objects.

No one has been able to "prove" beyond doubt that ghosts exist, just as it has been impossible to verify the existence of UFOs, the Abominable Snowman, or the Loch Ness Monster. Those who deride the notion of ghosts echo the words of Ebenezer Scrooge when he said Marley's ghost was only "a slight disorder of the stomach . . . an undigested bit of beef, a blot of mustard, a crumb of cheese, a fragment of an underdone potato."

Are the stories on the following pages true? We can't "prove" their accuracy. However, we believe that the participants in the stories *believe* sincerely in what happened to them. The people you will read about, and the writers of this book, cannot explain the events. Nor have we tried. We are reporting what happened. We have tried to present the stories in a nonjudgmental way, leaving it up to you, the reader, to draw your own conclusions.

Alas, there are no truly famous or prominent ghosts among the five dozen stories we've collected. As far as we know, there is no ghost permanently ensconced in the governor's mansion, no ephemeral actresses still trodding the boards of abandoned theaters long after death, and no phantom cavalry troop still parading at Fort McCoy. But many of the ghosts that follow are (or have been) very much in evidence. Some historical ghosts attracted the attention of newspapers in their day, and their shenanigans were widely reported.

Professor Robert Gard, the noted Wisconsin folklorist, has said that Wisconsin may have more ghosts per square mile than any other state. We emphatically agree!

There is an amazing collection of haunted houses, poltergeists, apparitions, and other unexplainable phenomena in a state known more for its cheese and vacation resorts.

The specters and stories you'll encounter include:

• the Ridgeway ghost, which has mystified residents of the wind-choked valleys of southwestern Wisconsin for 150 years;

• a possessed servant girl in early Milwaukee;

• the lingering specter of a long-dead woman in a house her husband built;

• a flamboyant grandmother who came back as a ghost to check up on the relatives;

• a poltergeist in St. Croix County that attracted a crowd of over three hundred spectators;

• two sisters who share a strange ability to attract representatives of the spirit world;

• two Ojibway ghosts that visited an Indian family one winter day and stayed for a month;

• a gentle southern lady who came back to help her descendant find missing branches on the family tree;

• several spirits that refused to leave some early Wisconsin hostelries, even after the inns were shuttered;

• a phantom horse that signaled death during the pioneer days of the Wisconsin Dells region;

• a ghost that takes its *modus operandi* from the fertile imagination of Washington Irving;

• a German-born farmer who returns to his tragedy-plagued farm near Waukesha even today;

• the strange events in a Cedarburg house that drove a young family to the brink of hysteria; and

• the ghost of a devoted wife who returned nineteen years after her death on the very night her husband died.

You will read about not only ghosts and apparitions but mysterious footsteps in the night, swinging railroad lanterns held by unseen hands, sounds that defy explanation, and a house that would burst into flame for no earthly reason. There is even a case of demonic possession, which ended only after the ancient rite of exorcism was performed in a Watertown church.

We have often been asked what prompted our interest in the ghosts of Wisconsin. Our objectives in writing the book were threefold. First, we wanted to entertain, to offer compelling stories that would engage the imagination. Second, we sought to fill a niche in the state's folklore/historical legacy by writing on a subject that had never before been covered in detail. Perhaps this skein of tales, woven into the fabric of Wisconsin's history, will give us a firmer appreciation of our regional character. And, last, we wanted to contribute to the vast body of ghost lore extant, with the hope that some of our stories might be significant.

Because no body of research existed for us to draw upon, we created our own. We wrote to nearly every newspaper in the state, inviting readers with information on ghost lore to tell us their stories. We also contacted selected county historical societies and every student newspaper in the University of Wisconsin System. The responses were encouraging, both in quantity and quality. Where possible we interviewed respondents in order to tape-record their stories. We were impressed by the sincerity of the people we interviewed, by their willingness to share with us their experiences. On numerous occasions we were told that we were the first persons, outside the immediate family, to hear the story. The fear of ridicule and derision prevented the telling to others. We vividly remember one young woman who was so traumatized by the recounting of the unexplainable events that her hands trembled as she served us coffee. And this was four years after the haunting!

Where time or distance made personal interviews difficult, we mailed detailed questionnaires to the subjects in order to evaluate their material.

Other contemporary and historical tales included in this book were gleaned from many sources. We consulted the Manuscript Collection at the State Historical Society of Wisconsin; city, county, and state histories; copies of nineteenth- and early twentieth-century newspapers; books and magazines of folklore and parapsychology. We excluded from consideration most material centering upon the famous Spiritualist Movement in Wisconsin, feeling that it was beyond the scope of this book.

Any book is the result of numerous contributions. We received assistance from many sources, some of whom prefer to remain anonymous. We wish to acknowledge the help that the following people provided:

Tim Ericson, archivist at the Area Research Center of the University of Wisconsin at River Falls, for his invaluable bibliographic insights and encouragement;

Paul Woehrmann, Milwaukee Public Library; Willis Miller, editor, *Hudson Star-Observer*; Jim Bednarek, writer-photographer, *Germantown Press*; Betsy Doehlert, free-lance writer, Madison; Tom Heinen, reporter, *Milwaukee Journal*; Jeanie Lewis, author of *Ridgeway Host to the Ghost*, and C. W. Orton, two indefatigable pursuers of the Ridgeway ghost; Marjorie M. Davies, librarian, Kilbourn Public Library, Wisconsin Dells; Mrs. Verne Worthing, Evansville; Richard Heiden, Milwaukee; Ervin Kontowicz, Milwaukee; and the dozens of people who told us their ghost stories and without whom this book would have been impossible. Most of all we would like to thank our editor, Mark E. Lefebvre, for his wise guidance and unfailing enthusiasm.

We hope that you have as much fun reading about haunted Wisconsin as we have had chasing the ghosts from the coulees to the farms, from the wooded northland to the city streets. Elusive creatures they are—we never met a single one! At least, we don't think so.

Beth Scott
J. Michael Norman

September 1980

Grateful acknowledgment is made to Branden Press, Boston, for permission to adapt material from **Tomorrows Unlimited**, *by Marion Stresau, copyright 1973, by Branden Press, Inc.*

The names of some individuals have been fictionalized to protect their privacy. These names are indicated by an asterisk (*) the first time they appear.

Part I.
The Haunted North

THE SPIRITS OF MADELINE ISLAND

Before white men came to Wisconsin there was a land called *Moningwunakaunig*, "place of the golden-breasted woodpecker." We call it Madeline, largest of the Apostle Islands scattered off Lake Superior's shore near Bayfield.

Madeline Island is a fourteen-thousand-acre refuge with white sand beaches hugging impenetrable forests of fir, spruce, pine, and hardwoods and contrasting sharply with wind-sculpted red granite cliffs on the island's lake side. It is an ancient place. For three thousand years Madeline has known human footsteps. Primitive peoples camped in the forests, taking from the waters and forests their simple diet of fish, meat, and berries when Roman armies were conquering Europe.

Later, the Ojibway (Chippewa) were forced from their ancestral home along the St. Lawrence River and settled on the Apostle Islands. A great village was built on Madeline with a population, archeologists say, of nearly twelve thousand. But the area became overpopulated and a terrible famine struck the Chippewa people.

Farming was rudimentary, if practiced at all; the men of the tribe could not kill enough fish and game to feed a village the size of a small modern city. In desperation, tribal elders and the medicine men resorted to cannibalism. Young maidens and children were chosen and offered as sacrifices on a primitive altar, their flesh used as food. But, the population rebelled after a time and the old leadership was executed.

Tales began spreading that the island was haunted by the vengeful spirits of the dead women and children. They would rise from the earth near the sacrificial altar and wander over the island.

Legend says a great exodus took place and the entire village was evacuated to the mainland until not a Chippewa remained on Madeline. Various families migrated to locations in northern Wisconsin and Minnesota. Some accounts insist it was several centuries before the Chippewa would again camp on the large island.

Now there are few Indians on the island. Earlier in this century, it is said, some sacrificial tobacco was found scattered at the site of the ancient altar.

Today Madeline Island caters primarily to tourists and several hundred residents. Few traces remain of the island's original inhabitants. A modern yacht harbor and marina occupy the lagoon near which the sacrificial altar was located. Nearby is a lavish resort and a golf course created in 1967 by the world-famous designer

Indian burial ground, Madeline Island

Robert Trent Jones. A few old islanders say the lagoon used to harbor the ghosts of those killed and devoured centuries ago. Although no one has reported any recent apparitions, on a cool, dark, foggy night if you sit near the shore of that lagoon, at the edge of the old Indian burial ground, and listen intently you might hear the haunting, plaintive cries of the sacrificed.

Two Ojibway Ghosts

In ancient days, Indians roamed Wisconsin. Game was plentiful in the dense forests, and men, hunting each day, provided well for their families.

One winter evening, a young Ojibway wife, awaiting the return of her husband, became uneasy. He was always home earlier, tired but eager to sit by the fire and spin stories of the day's adventures for her and the child. But now?

Suddenly the silence of the night was broken by the sound of footsteps. The wife hurried to the door of the lodge. Her husband was nowhere in sight. Instead, two strange women stood beyond the doorway, their thin figures wrapped in garments that almost concealed their long, hollow-eyed faces. The hunter's wife did not recognize them. They were not of her tribe and she had no idea where they might have come from. The nearest family lived a distance of several days' travel through the woods. Yet, not wishing to appear inhospitable, she invited them in to warm up by the fire. They accepted her invitation but, instead of going to the fire, huddled in a dark corner of the room.

Suddenly a voice cried out, "Merciful spirit, there are two corpses clothed in garments!" The wife wheeled around. There was no one there, no one except the silent guests. Had she been dreaming? Hearing only the sound of a rising wind?

Then the door burst open and the hunter appeared, dragging behind him the carcass of a large, fat deer. At that instant, the strangers rushed to the animal and began pulling off the choicest bits of white fat. The husband and wife, although astonished by such impropriety, decided that their guests must be famished and so they said nothing.

The next day when the hunter returned from the chase, the same thing occurred.

On the third day, the young man, deciding to cater to the whims of his peculiar visitors, tied a bundle of fat on the top of the carcass he brought home. The women seized it eagerly, then ate the portion of fat that had been set aside for the wife. The hunter, although tempted to rebuke them, remained silent. For some mysterious reason he had had unaccountable good luck in bringing down game since the ghostly visitors had come into his home; he thought that perhaps somehow his good fortune had something to do with their presence. Besides, the women didn't cause any trouble; on the contrary, they began to be helpful. Each evening they gathered wood, stacked it by the fire, and returned all implements to the place where they had found them. During the daytime, they huddled unobtrusively in a corner. They never joined a family conversation, nor laughed or joked.

Finally, one evening in early spring, the hunter stayed out later than usual. When he did appear with a carcass, the visitors tore off the fat so rudely that the wife, who had held her anger in check for so many months, was on the verge of lashing out at the usurpers. Although she managed to keep silent, she was certain, this time, that the guests sensed her resentment.

After the family had gone to bed, the husband heard the women weeping. He tried to sleep, but their sobbing seemed incessant. Recalling the looks exchanged between his wife and the guests, he worried that his mate had offended them. Had she spoken sharply to them? Said something that he perhaps hadn't heard? He got up, went over to the women, and asked what was wrong. After assuring him that he had treated them kindly, they spoke further.

"We come from the land of the dead to test the sincerity of the living," they began. They explained that many living people, bereaved by death in a family, say that if only the dead could be restored to life they would devote the rest of their lives to making them happy. The Master of Life had given them "three moons" in which to test the sincerity of those who had lost friends or relatives. "We have been here more than half that time," they said, "but now your wife is so angered by our presence that we have decided we must leave."

The hunter's wife, awakened now by the voices, arose and stood at her husband's side. The ghosts went on to explain why they had eaten the choicest parts of the hunter's kills. "That was the particular trial selected for you. We know, by your customs, that the white fat is reserved for the wife. In usurping that privilege we have put you both to a severe test of your tempers and feelings. But that is what we were sent to do."

Before the astonished hunter and his wife could respond, the ghosts blessed them and said good-bye.

At that moment, the lodge was plunged into total darkness. The couple heard the door open and shut. The ghosts had gone. But their blessings were made manifest in the years to come. The hunter excelled in the chase, fathered many splendid children, and enjoyed health, wealth, and a long life. Such were the rewards of befriending two lonely ghosts who had come to test him on a winter's night of long ago.

THE BURNINGS

In the middle of the nineteenth century, Norwegians from southeastern Wisconsin began moving into the sandy jack-pine area of northwestern Wisconsin. Here, in the harsh and isolated Indianhead country, the new immigrants broke the land and attempted to wrest a living from the poor soil.

One family had just finished building a snug house and had moved in. Returning home late one evening, they discovered that a window curtain was burned black. The ashes lay on the floor, which, strangely, was not burned. There was no sign of fire anywhere else in the house. Although perplexed, they soon put the event out of mind.

A year later the family returned and smelled smoke upon entering the house. They soon discovered that a chair cushion was smoldering. Again, they were at a loss to find a cause, and a search of the house revealed no other fires—everything was in order.

The next year they returned home from a visit and found their house burned to the ground. They rebuilt it.

The following year, a fire broke out in the middle of the night and the family members, all sleeping upstairs, were barely able to escape. Feeling lucky to be alive and not wishing to tempt fate further, they abandoned the ruins.

Many years later, a newcomer to the area bought the land and planned to build a summer cabin on it. Construction was partway along when the carpenter, arriving one morning to resume work, found the charred remains of his apron on the floor exactly where he had left it the previous day. It was thought that the structure had not caught fire because it was of green lumber. About this time the stranger learned the history of the place, paid off the workman, and fled.

What started the mysterious fires? If they had been of incendiary origin, why didn't the house burn down the first time or the second time? If the occupants had been targeted for destruction, why did a fire break out on the site many years later, after they had left the area?

Were the burnings only coincidence, or was a supernatural force at work? The history of ghost lore is filled with accounts of spontaneous fires—flames igniting clothing in closets, burning mattresses on unoccupied beds, and fires erupting in the center of bare floors. All are thought to be the work of a poltergeist—an unseen ghost who smashes dishes, moves furniture, and, in its most malevolent mood, starts fires.

Was this the case here? Or was it something else?

THE COULEE ROAD GHOST

Hudson, Wisconsin, is a small, bustling city clinging to the bluffs of the St. Croix River. The city is a popular suburban home for workers in Minneapolis/St. Paul, Minnesota, only fifteen miles to the west. Its scenic river beauty, coupled with pleasant small-town living, makes it a popular locale. Nothing much out of the ordinary happens in Hudson . . . except the legendary visits by the ghost of Paschal Aldrich.

The story of the hauntings on what is now called Coulee Road begins nearly a hundred forty years ago with the arrival in Hudson of one of its first residents, Dr. Philip Aldrich.

Aldrich, who was born in Ohio in 1792, could justifiably be called a pioneer entrepreneur. He became over the years a businessman, mail carrier and postmaster, county commissioner, circuit judge, and landowner. No doubt the ease with which he accomplished these tasks was due in some measure to the small population of St. Croix County in 1845—1,419 inhabitants. That was according to Dr. Aldrich's own census! In those days, the county included most of northwestern Wisconsin and that part of Minnesota between the Mississippi River and St. Croix River.

Shortly after Aldrich arrived in the county in 1840, the federal government awarded him a contract to carry twice-monthly mail dispatches from Point Douglas to St. Croix Falls. During the summer he piloted a flat-bottomed river boat, called a bateau, and in the winter he trod the ice-covered river by foot.

Two years later, Dr. Aldrich was elected a

county commissioner and continued to be closely associated with the political growth of western Wisconsin for many years. According to newspaper accounts, the first meeting of the St. Croix County Board was held September 9, 1848, at the home of Dr. Aldrich, which stood at the northeast corner of Second Street and Elm in Hudson. The house was a center of many gala social events in early Hudson.

Dr. Aldrich had moved into Hudson during the previous year, 1847. He bought a large tract of land, now called the Aldrich Addition. Aldrich abandoned his mail route via the St. Croix River, and an overland route was begun from Hudson to St. Croix Falls. The mail was delivered on foot once a week, a distance of some eighty miles round trip!

In 1849, Aldrich became Hudson's first postmaster, a position he held until 1851. In that same year he was also granted a license to operate a ferry across the St. Croix River.

The Paschal Aldrich Home

A son of Dr. Aldrich, Paschal, owned a home on Buckeye Street that became the first post office. Paschal's wife, Martha, often clerked in the post office and since she could neither read nor write, the patrons picked out their own letters.

Following Dr. Philip Aldrich's death, the large holdings were passed on to Paschal. But the luck of the father was not invested in the son.

Paschal Aldrich and his family moved to a small house at the head of Coulee Road, near present Interstate Highway 94. He farmed a large area for many years, but when a serious illness altered his fortunes he was forced to sell much of the property. There is some dispute as to the reason for the sale. One newspaper account reports that an unidentified man somehow caused the family to lose its vast holdings during Paschal's illness.

Paschal Aldrich died on October 13, 1860, in that house on Coulee Road. For years afterward, the place was known as the "haunted house." Members of his family and some neighbors said they saw Paschal's ghost wandering the premises at night, reportedly keeping watch over his family. Paschal's solicitude in death was attributed to his near financial ruin during the illness preceding his death.

Mrs. Paschal Aldrich also vowed to come back in the form of a ghost. But her granddaughter, the late Mrs. Wallace Smith, said, "I've never heard if there was ever a second ghost out there or not."

Perhaps one was enough.

THE CANTANKEROUS GHOST
OF ST. CROIX COUNTY

August 30, 1873, was a fine day for cutting hay, and St. Croix County farmer Richard Lynch welcomed assistance from his neighbor Frank Duffie. Side by side they worked, swinging their scythes in the sun-washed field at the hem of the forest.

At four o'clock, Mrs. Lynch screamed from the house. The men ran, reaching the log home in time to see chairs jumping to the ceiling and crashing to the floor, tinware and cooking utensils flying across the room and landing in a far corner. Beyond the open doorway, slabs of boards and scraps of iron sailed through the air.

The three rushed outside. Duffie, determined to catch the culprit, stationed himself at one corner of the house, with Lynch at the diagonal corner so that together they had a full view of all sides of the house. Duffie saw—no one.

Suddenly, a large pine box near Duffie leaped into the air and landed ten feet away on the porch. A moment later, an old horseshoe that had been hanging on a peg in the milkhouse arced through the air and came to rest beside the box. Instantly, a commotion rocked the empty house. The Lynches and their neighbor ran back inside. Everything movable had been piled high into one corner.

Later, a broadax that had been stuck into the end of a log by the milkhouse struck the side of the dwelling's doorway and bounded several feet into the room. Mrs. Lynch seized the ax, took it to the milkhouse, and jammed it into a box. She covered the box with slats and a bag of salt. No sooner had she returned to the house than the ax reappeared, this time settling on the porch. Her husband grabbed the ax, took it a short distance from the house, and pushed it into a hollow log. There it remained—at least for the rest of that day.

If Duffie was shaken by these manifestations, the Lynches were less so. Although this August afternoon was the first time that these Cady Township residents had actually seen objects flying from place to place, they'd been plagued by perplexing incidents since December of 1871.

In the latter part of that month, Mrs. Lynch began missing dresses. Some were found rolled and stuffed into odd nooks and crannies; others had been cut to shreds, suitable only for the ragbag. Two holes were cut in a feather bed. Dishes and pans disappeared, to be located later in unusual places. Sometimes Mrs. Lynch, while preparing a meal, would put down a utensil, look away for a moment, then find that the tool had vanished.

Immediate suspicion centered upon the four children: David, seventeen; Mary, ten; Georgie, seven; and Rena, two. All denied knowledge of the mischief, but Georgie, who had been caught in a number of childish pranks, was often spanked when anything was missing.

One day Lynch returned home from town with dress goods for his wife. She put the material away in the bedroom. Several days later when she went for it, it was gone. It was located finally in the barn, rolled into a bundle with the shears inside. From the cloth had been cut the skirt and sleeves of a dress to fit Mary.

A second bolt of material vanished also.

Weeks later it was found rolled into a hanging wall map. A perfect bib-type apron had been cut from the cloth.

The parents were stunned. They didn't think Georgie was responsible, but without proof they couldn't be certain.

Although only a few neighbors had known of these early bizarre incidents, news of the flying furniture and farm implements spread like a prairie fire. Area newsmen visited the Lynches to witness the poltergeist's activities, then vied with one another in recounting what one editor called "the most absurd capering of some supernatural agency."

Strangers, their imaginations sparked by what they read, converged upon the little homestead in the clearing. By foot, by horse, by rumbling ox-drawn wagon they came, winding their way through the nearly impenetrable forest known as the Big Woods. One newsman estimated that more than three hundred visitors had descended upon the Lynch family within a six-weeks period; another estimated a thousand visitors.

Meanwhile, the uneasy mother had begun binding Georgie hand and foot and tying him into a chair or cradle. One day while she was washing clothes, Georgie was tied into his cradle with Mary watching him. Mrs. Lynch turned from the washboard to put some wood into the stove. Turning back to the washtub, she found her bowl of soft soap gone. She went after more and, upon her return, Georgie told her the soap was under his head. The startled mother raised the child's head from the crib pillow and found the soap. Neither Georgie nor Mary could explain how it got there.

But it didn't seem to matter whether Georgie

was bound. Often, while the child was confined, a teacup would fly to the floor and smash, or a saucer would leap from the sideboard and land undamaged on the floor. Then Georgie would shout, "There, mother! You see I didn't do that!"

One incident greatly distressed Mrs. Lynch. Little Rena, the baby, had very beautiful hair. It hung in long, golden ringlets, of which her mother was naturally very proud. On a warm April day the little girl was playing on the porch in front of the house. The mother, finishing her work, went to check on her daughter. She gasped in horror. The child sat motionless on the porch and her hair was sheared as close to the scalp as it could be cut! The shears were found a few feet away, but not a single lock of hair was ever found.

On another day, Mrs. Lynch was cooking a kettle of squirrels for the family's midday meal. After cautioning Mary to watch the boiling pot, she took a pan to the milkhouse to get flour to make bread. She got the flour, sprinkled salt over it, then returned to the house. As she stepped into the doorway, she saw that the pot had disappeared from the stove. Mary claimed to know nothing of the pot's disappearance. Mrs. Lynch put the pan of flour on the table, then she, Mary, and Georgie began searching for the missing kettle.

Emerging from the bedroom, Mrs. Lynch saw that the pan of flour was gone. In a few moments it was discovered under the stairway; again it was placed on the table. Mother and children then went up to the garret and there, sitting in the middle of the bed, was the pot of squirrels. A corner of the bedspread had been thrown over the kettle. As Mrs. Lynch threw off the spread, the contents of the pot steamed and bubbled as if it were being lifted off the stove. The soot-blackened pot left no mark on the white sheet.

Returning to the kitchen, Mrs. Lynch found the pan of flour again missing. It was discovered later behind the milkhouse.

On another day, Mrs. Lynch went to the milkhouse for milk. She found each of the five pans of milk layered with soft soap. Stepping over to the soap barrel that stood in a corner, she noticed four or five impressions in the thick, pasty mass. Each bore the marks of a large, adult hand—a hand with three fingers!

Who did it? That's what *Dunn County News* publishers R. J. Flint and E. M. Weber wondered when they saw it. They wondered about a lot more too during their overnight visit to the mysterious house.

"Rock" Flint reported that Messrs. Thompson, Kendall, Johnson, and Burch, clerks in the Knapp, Stout and Company store, arrived later that night from Menomonie. Sunday morning after breakfast, Flint and some of the other men went outside in order to give the family a chance to finish up their work. The morning air was chilly and the visitors built a fire at the edge of the woods, about forty feet from the house.

Suddenly they heard a noise coming from inside the house, a thumping noise as if a heavy weight had fallen on the floor. Then another. Someone shouted that teacups were falling to the floor, striking the floor bottoms up, but not breaking.

Flint wrote, "Mr. Thompson, who was near the door, stepped forward and picked up the cup, placed it on the table, took Georgie, who was in the room, by the hand, and started for the door. In a moment another cup sped to the floor and lay on its side, whirling with great rapidity. Thompson started for this one, also, and as he grabbed it, the cup moved away from him and passed under the table. He went around to the other side and caught it while it was whirling. This transpired while we were at the fire, and we relate it substantially as it was told us by several eyewitnesses.

> "Planting ourselves in the doorway, we stood prepared to see something; we had not long to wait. With almost lightning swiftness an egg darted across the room, struck the corner of a box, and was smashed. Shortly after, the potato masher, which stood on the dresser, went the same way with incredible speed, and landed in the corner 'kerslap.' In a little while a couple of pieces of broken crockery lying on the stove made a sudden change of pace and landed in the corner.
>
> "These three things we saw distinctly, and others in the room saw them. Perhaps we were fooled by some trick of legerdemain. If so, who did it? The boy seven years old who sat at the table quietly eating his breakfast? The girl, ten years old, who stood nearby, wiping a dish? Mrs. Lynch, who was busy at work? Or Mr. Lynch, who was not in the house? It seems to us improbable, if not impossible."

Yet the impossible events increased daily. Shortly after the newsmen's visit, the Lynches hosted A. B. Finley, school superintendent of Barron County. He too stayed all night and that night, for the first time, disturbances occurred in the house after the family had retired. All slept in the same bedroom—Mr. Lynch and his wife and Rena in one bed; Finley in a bed across the room; and Mary and Georgie sleeping in a bed on the floor between the other beds.

Soon after they had retired, Georgie complained of something pinching and scratching him. Finley took Georgie into his own bed, but still the child complained. The guest then clamped the boy's hands in one of his own and put his other arm so tightly around him that Georgie could not move a muscle without detection. All was still. Suddenly Finley felt the bedclothes stirring. He swatted, he grabbed, and caught—nothing. The stirrings continued far into the night, leaving the superintendent, by dawn, thoroughly exhausted and thoroughly baffled.

Not so baffled was a reporter from the *St. Paul Dispatch* who visited the Lynches on November 3 and 4, 1873. When curious scratching noises emitted from the children's bed during his all-night visit, he got up, pulled on his pants, and held the hands of both children. The noises stopped immediately. The reporter, after spending twenty hours in the house, went away convinced that Mrs. Lynch and ten-year-old Mary, whom he called "strange and precocious," had duped people. He felt that Mrs. Lynch was bored and unhappy in her dreary, backwoods home and that, after her husband's refusal to sell the farm and move back east, she created her own excitement. Also, because the remote location of the Lynch home meant that most visitors had to spend the night, the newsman felt that many guests paid much more for the hospitality than they would have paid in a commercial hostelry. The reporter saw the setup as a money-making scheme that Mrs. Lynch didn't want to relinquish.

The majority of observers, however, continued to believe that the Lynches would have

3

relinquished almost anything to be rid of the manifestations, that they were victims rather than perpetrators of the havoc wrought.

When Mr. Knight and Mr. Coen—two gentlemen who lived near the Wilson railroad station—visited the house, the "spirits" were especially lively. While articles flew around the room, Knight took a sheet of paper and wrote down each occurrence as it happened. In the few hours the two men were there, Knight recorded more than forty different manifestations. One time the potato masher flew from the cupboard and hit the floor on the opposite side of the room. Knight picked it up, replaced it on the cupboard, and remarked that he'd like to see them do that again. No family member was near the cupboard. Knight had scarcely seated himself when the masher zipped through the air and splintered a mirror.

About that time, Mrs. Lynch had finished grinding coffee in a portable mill. She replaced the mill on a shelf and crossed the room to get something. As she walked away, the drawer of the coffee mill, partly filled with ground coffee, came out of the mill and followed, airborne, two feet behind her. One of the men sprang forward to catch the drawer, but it fell to the floor upside down. Until she heard it strike the floor, Mrs. Lynch had no knowledge of the drawer's movement.

On another morning, Ambrose Evans visited the Lynches. When breakfast was ready, he sat down at the table. Every member of the family was present. Soon, the distinctive odor of kerosene filled the air. It seemed to be coming from the bedroom, whose door was open. Evans followed Mrs. Lynch into the room. There, in the middle of the bed, lay a jug of oil, uncorked. Nearly a gallon of oil had emptied upon the bed, saturating the feather bed and the quilts.

When *Milwaukee News* correspondent J. D. Goodrich arrived at the house, the oldest boy and his father were working in a field and the younger children were outside playing. Goodrich was standing by the outdoor cellar talking to Mrs. Lynch when a noise erupted from inside the house.

"There," said Mrs. Lynch. "You hear that, and you also see that none of the family are in the house."

Hurrying inside, Goodrich and his hostess found the table tipped over.

By eight-thirty the next morning things got livelier. Goodrich wrote, "One thing peculiar is that you never see a thing start, but the minute you turn your eyes the thing gets up and gets. Another peculiar feature is that where a thing strikes there it lays, neither rolls nor bounds. We took some of the same things and threw them a number of times, but they would bound or roll every time. We saw a piece of broken cup hit a little two-year-old girl on the back so hard she nearly cried. A raw potato hopped out of a dish near where we were and lit on the floor; and while we were watching a stove handle light in one place, a tin plate whisked by our head in another direction."

The Reverend John Barker, who lived on Cady Creek in Pierce County, was convinced that the devil was at work in the Lynch household. Bent upon exorcising the demon, he approached his neighbor's house with Bible and prayer book. Tying the two books into a handkerchief, he placed them on the stairway, then challenged the spirit to remove them.

But something caused the minister to divert his eyes. When he looked again, the books were gone. After a lengthy search, they were found on a bed. Every leaf had been shaken out of the Bible. And the handkerchief was found in a barrel of feathers. As Barker gazed in astonishment, a broadax came whirling through the doorway and struck at his feet. Positive that someone had thrown it, he vowed to catch the prankster. After the ax had been placed in a trunk, Barker and the family members rushed outside. They saw no one. Upon their return, they found the ax standing by the door, resting on the blade.

The dumbfounded old gentleman stepped cautiously around the room, never taking his eyes from the ax. Suddenly it started toward him, rolling over and over. The white-faced minister asked his hosts if he might offer a prayer. No sooner was the amen spoken than pictures, maps, and clocks flew from the walls. Barker fled.

It was about this time that the family Bible disappeared. After a lengthy search, it was found in a kettle of water above the stove, sandwiched between an apron and a tea canister.

Meanwhile, as visitors filled the house, one fatuous braggart announced that he had two hundred dollars in his wallet that the spirit could have if it could take it. Within five minutes the money was gone—forever.

If the casual observer could offer no explanation for the manifestations he witnessed, neither could the spiritualists and mediums who besieged the Lynch home after Lynch offered fifty dollars to any psychic who could duplicate the poltergeist's activities. None could, nor could they explain the mystery.

One Saturday afternoon a clairvoyant named Mellon, from Rock Elm in Pierce County, visited the Lynches. He saw nothing that day of an otherworldly nature. The next day he had better luck. He told Lynch that he saw the spirit of Lynch's first wife, that she and six other spirits were the cause of all the disturbances. When Lynch asked why so many things had been destroyed, Mellon said that it was to open the minds of the Lynch family and the minds of others in the community to the truths of spiritualism. Lynch grumbled that it seemed a questionable and expensive way to gain converts to the faith.

A large group had gathered and someone asked Mellon if the spirits could throw things around as they had done previously. The answer was yes. Lynch then asked them to move a cup from its shelf to the floor. The cup did not move. The spirit, speaking through Mellon, said that it was alone and could not perform without the assistance of the other spirits. Where were the other spirits? They had gone to Knapp Station, some twelve miles away, to attend a camp meeting. The spirit could not tell when they would return and finally agreed to go after them. The medium then announced that the spirit had departed and that there was no telling when it would come back. Visitors muttered "humbug" and shuffled away.

Some time later, Mrs. Carlton, a clairvoyant from River Falls, visited the Lynches. She too saw seven spirits. She advised the family to keep all visitors away and to hold seances among themselves, during which the mystery would be explained through the mediumship of someone in the family. Lynch, although skeptical, gave it a try. During several family circles the table moved about, but all attempts at questioning proved abortive and the family gave up spiritualism in disgust.

In the latter part of October the manifestations became more violent and more destructive than at any previous period. One day while Mrs. Lynch and Mary were alone in the house, the table started across the room, bounded to the ceiling and back to the floor, then hit the side of the room hard enough to split one of the leaves. In a final defiant gesture, it leaped into the air and crashed to the floor with such force that the entire top was wrenched from the frame.

Surveying his property losses—smashed furniture, broken dishes, mangled silverware, shattered mirrors and clocks, shredded clothing—Lynch regretted ever bringing his family out of Marshall County, Indiana, two years ago. Exhausted by the discomfort and inconvenience of sharing his small house day and night with curious strangers, and desperate to put an end to the activities of the unseen ghost, he made a bold decision. Announcing that he was splitting up the family, he promptly bundled Mary and Georgie off to the McMahans, neighbors living a mile away.

With the children's departure, peace settled upon the Lynch household. From that day on, no unusual occurrences were reported at either house. Are there rational explanations for this story? Possibly. If, as one reporter thought, Mrs. Lynch was retaliating against her husband for his refusal to sell the farm, couldn't she have enlisted Mary's help in performing some of the "mysterious" feats? Together, or singly, the women could have cut the dress material or punched holes in the feather bed. Couldn't Mrs. Lynch have encouraged the children to hide pots and pans and kitchen utensils? Did Mary grab the bowl of soap while her mother's back was turned, then put it under Georgie's head when Mrs. Lynch left the room to get more soap? Did she also put the kettle of squirrels on the bed in the garret? Stir up the bedclothes to keep Georgie and Finley awake all night? Or cut her little sister's hair?

Yet, if we attribute these activities to human intervention, what of the other manifestations—the objects that flew around almost daily for a period of two months?

The fact that all disturbances ceased after the children were removed to the neighbors' house doesn't prove that they had anything to do with it, at least not on a conscious level. Parapsychologists say that the mysterious movements of objects are often associated with the presence of young children and, more frequently, by the presence of teen-agers. It is thought that the turbulence and energy force of the teen-ager are somehow transferred to inanimate objects. The one teen-ager in the family, David, was mentioned only once in the news accounts, when Goodrich reported that the older boy was working in the field with his father. If, in fact, David had "hired out" to work for neighboring farmers, as was the custom for boys of his age at that time, could his psyche have remained behind to create the havoc? Or was Georgie the focus for the levitations, as some experts believe? Questions without answers.

Today, the log house and the Big Woods in Cady Township are gone. Silos dwarf white clapboard farmhouses near the once-thriving village of Hatchville, and fields unroll to the horizon. The remarkable story of the Lynch family stays alive only in the musty files of newspapers.

THE CHIEFTAIN'S CURSE

The haunted house of legend must be a stately old mansion perched atop a windswept knoll. One enters the grounds through a gate attached by a single hinge to the decrepit fence winding around the property. The building is in a desperate state of disrepair—planks missing from the front veranda, windows boarded up or broken—and, for good measure, a few bats ought to flutter from one of the gable windows. Of course, one visits the mansion at midnight when it is cold and windy, and terror seems to wait just beyond that large, forbidding door.

Well, that's fiction. In fact, one of Wisconsin's more famous haunted houses fits only part of that imaginary picture. In earlier days this house and the land upon which it still stands seemed to be cursed with evil. No fewer than ten people associated with the mansion met unusual deaths. Although there have been no reports of rattling chains or ghostly apparitions, if a house can be haunted with grief and sorrow it is the Scott mansion in Merrill.

In the early part of the last century an Indian village occupied the west bank of the Wisconsin River in what is now the city of Merrill. French fur traders had often stopped at the village to barter for goods. The peaceful Indians had little fear of the white men. When lumbermen began traveling the river during the big timber drives in northern Wisconsin they were welcomed as brothers by the inhabitants.

The village chief would bring the visitors to his wigwam where they would be served meals by his only daughter. The men were entranced by the beautiful, shy maiden who soon became known as Jenny to her white guests. But the blissful life of the settlement soon turned to tragedy. A young lumberjack who was particularly fond of Jenny made love to her. The accounts differ as to what happened next. One version asserts that Jenny, ashamed of her act, killed herself. Another tale states that Jenny simply died soon thereafter, probably of the flu, which had been introduced among the Indian peoples by the white men.

Whatever the cause of lovely Jenny's death, her father was grief-stricken. He ordered that she be buried upon a high hill across the river from the settlement. At her burial the old man stood at his daughter's grave, gazed out over the river, and prayed, "Oh, great Father, grant me this place for my child. Let this ground be sacred to her memory." Then he placed a curse upon that earth: "Let it never do any white man any good."

The years passed, the Indians abandoned the settlement, and Jenny and her final resting place were all but forgotten. The village that had grown beside the Indian camp was named to honor S. S. Merrill, the manager of the St. Paul railroad.

But in 1884 there began a series of events so strange that the old chief's grim incantation seemed to echo down through the ages.

T. B. Scott, a wealthy Merrill mill owner and lumberman, purchased "Jenny's hill" from the government and there planned to build a mansion fit for a timber baron. He knew nothing of Jenny or the curse. Only two years after he bought the land, in 1886, Scott died with the house only partially built. He was fifty-seven. Scott's widow, Ann, in ill health, tried to complete construction of the mansion. But within a year Ann was dead. It was now left to their son, Walter, to finish his father's work.

Although his mother had urged him to

The Merrill House

complete the house, Walter apparently abandoned the project. Some years later, however, Walter did visit Chicago to consult an architect. During their meeting, Walter and the architect, a Mr. Sheldon, got into a fight and young Scott was stabbed to death with a letter opener. Sheldon proved self-defense, implying that Walter Scott instigated the struggle.

The Scott estate sold the still-uncompleted mansion to a Chicago millionaire, Mr. Kuechle. He wanted the house as a summer retreat and made plans to install lavish additions to the mansion. Kuechle visited the World's Columbian Exposition in Chicago in 1893 and bought a number of decorations for the house, including heavy, hand-carved doors, plate glass windows, embossed mirrors, and a carved mantel. He hired workmen to install the furnishings and complete the construction. Kuechle apparently spent little if any time in the mansion. Within a short time, a series of bad investments forced him to mortgage the house to a Chicago tavern owner named Barsanti. Kuechle was able to avoid foreclosure on the mansion when he inherited a large sum of money. Determined to recoup his losses, Kuechle invested the fortune in a contract to build a section of the Northern Pacific Railroad. The man knew nothing of railroads or engineering, soon went bankrupt, and later died in a mental institution.

Barsanti took possession but never lived to see the mansion. He had apparently antagonized a murderous gang known as the Black Hand, and as he waited in Chicago's Union Station to board a train for Merrill he was stabbed to death by one of the "Hands."

The Barsanti family, in turn, sold the still-vacant and only half-completed mansion to a real estate speculator, George Gibson. His idea was to build a home for elderly lawyers. An office was organized in Merrill to collect donations, and work once again resumed on the mansion.

Late one afternoon Gibson left his office for home and supper and then he vanished. Search parties were organized to scour the countryside. The Wisconsin River was dragged without success. River banks and booms (sections of the river where freshly cut timber jam up) were carefully watched. There was no apparent motive for Gibson's sudden disappearance. He was a devoted family man, well liked by the townspeople, with no financial problems. Indeed, he had looked forward to the day when the mansion would house the aged barristers. But George Gibson was never seen alive or dead after that day.

The mansion reverted to the Barsanti family since all payments on the house had not been made. The family retained possession for several years during which the mansion was never occupied. A reputation of evil was now firmly attached to the old place. Caretakers looked after the house and grounds, mainly to protect it from vandals. One old groundsman was an Englishman called Popcorn Dan, since he also operated a popcorn stand in Merrill. In 1911 he sailed for England and a visit to his childhood home. Returning to America in 1912, however, he made a fatal mistake. Popcorn Dan booked passage on the S.S. *Titanic*.

The Lloydsen family became the mansion's caretakers after Popcorn Dan's death. Mr. Lloydsen died of alcoholism.

Finally, Mrs. Mary Fehlhaber, a Merrill area midwife, bought the mansion for a small sum and took in boarders. One day, while out riding, she became ill, made her way to a nearby farm home, but died before a doctor could reach her side.

In 1919, Herman Fehlhaber, Mary's husband, gave the house and adjoining property to the city of Merrill. Four years later the city gave the property to the Sisters of Mercy of the Holy Cross, an order of Roman Catholic nuns. The Scott mansion is now used as a residence for the sisters, who operate a hospital and small college nearby. Nothing peculiar has happened to the house or its occupants since 1923.

Is it only a macabre coincidence that so many people associated with the house met with tragedy during their lives? Or did that curse pronounced so very long ago carry through the decades to torment those who tried to build on "Jenny's hill"? Perhaps now that the mansion and the grounds are being used for humanitarian purposes there is peace on that high knoll.

Should you ever see the Scott mansion at the south end of Merrill, think of Jenny. Is the curse over? Yes, at least for now.

THE GIRL IN WHITE

In the early days of the twentieth century, few persons in rural Wisconsin traveled by car or even by buggy. Those who owned horses rode them; those less fortunate walked. John Groat was among the latter. One hot summer evening, he and his friend Ed, who also lived in the vicinity of Menomonie, walked the mile and a half to town. On the way back they decided to visit their girlfriends, Carrie and Anna. The girls were sisters and lived, with their parents, in a farmhouse not far from the road and a small stream.

As the men reached the wooden bridge that carried the highway over this shallow stream, they stopped briefly to reconsider their plans. Was it too late to visit the girls? After all, they weren't expected.

Before they could decide, Ed shouted, "Look, John! There's a girl all in white coming down the road." She came directly toward them, but turned at the bridge, walked down into the stream, and vanished.

Was it Carrie? Anna? How could anyone disappear in such a shallow body of water? Was there a deep hole some place?

After John and Ed recovered from their astonishment, they dashed to the spot where they had last seen the girl. They entered the water, walked back and forth, around and around, but could find no hole nor any trace of the girl. Where had she gone? Why, in fact, had she not crossed the bridge? Had the men's presence perhaps frightened her?

Knowing that the occurrence must be reported, John insisted that they stop at the farmhouse, which was only about eighty feet from this part of the stream. He feared that the girl in white must have been either Carrie or Anna, and he knew, without asking, that Ed shared that fear.

At the farmhouse, the girls' parents were still out on the porch. The mother explained that they had had company earlier and that the girls were now in the kitchen washing dishes.

     Carrie and Anna soon came out and listened to their boyfriends' story. Both girls said they had waded the stream many times and that there were no deep holes anywhere in it.

     Who or what had the men seen? No one knows. But afterward John always said that he would never have told the story if Ed had not been with him to witness that summer night's walk of the mysterious girl in white.

A QUARTET OF WISPS

Will-o'-the-wisp: *n.* A phosphorescent light that hovers over swampy ground at night, possibly caused by rotting organic matter.

     That is what the dictionary says, but Wisconsin pioneers often placed the will-o'-the-wisp in the same category as ghosts. Within the vast, dark forests, along river banks and lowlands, the eerie dancing lights would be seen moving and jumping as if they were living, breathing creatures. No theory about "possible rotting organic matter" could dissuade those hardy settlers that anything but the devil could be the culprit.

THE WISP THAT ROARED

     Mrs. Adele Cline of Eau Pleine recalls that the lights had the appearance of a man walking along in the dark swinging a lantern, a common method of travel in the early days. Mrs. Cline's father first saw the phenomenon on a homestead near the Big Eau Pleine

River in the 1880s. The first encounter took place one night on his way home from a visit to his parents' farm about a mile from his own cabin. The will-o'-the-wisp suddenly appeared beside him and followed him nearly to his doorstep.

Mrs. Cline's parents eventually built a barn on the land and surrounded the yard with a timber fence. The will-o'-the-wisp never entered the yard once the fence was erected.

The family homestead was quite near a small lake formed by the Big Eau Pleine River. Between the barn and lake was a large area covered by rock and slabs of stone. The children used to call it "the acre of stone." All around this section the land was cleared and under cultivation. Mrs. Cline said the light would come up from the river and cross over this stony expanse usually at twilight, although her mother watched as two lights chased each other until the early morning hours.

The light would sometimes travel very fast, "as though it was really in a hurry," while at other times it would hover and then slowly fade. A few minutes later it might reappear hundreds of feet away and continue its strange, nocturnal gyrations.

On one occasion Mrs. Cline's young aunt, twelve years old, and an uncle, who was only nine, came to visit the family. The children had been assigned the job of bringing in the livestock. Twilight descended and the youngsters had yet to complete their tasks. As they walked across a pasture the will-o'-the-wisp appeared floating beside them. Their dog took a look at the apparition and bolted for home. He hid for several days under the front porch. The cows also wasted little time in returning to the comforts of the barn.

A few days later Mrs. Cline's grandfather was returning home at dusk when he saw the glowing, bobbing will-o'-the-wisp. At the same instant a thunderous roar bellowed from deep within the earth. The old man had been a soldier in the German Kaiser's East Prussian Army. He was familiar with the roar of cannon fire, yet the sound on that night was more frightening than anything he had ever heard.

Could there have been an underground landslide in an impenetrable cavern? Was there a minor earthquake? The same sound was heard several years later by a neighbor boy returning along the same path. From that night on he carried a gun whenever he was out late.

Mrs. Cline's family eventually moved to an adjoining farm and their original homestead was rented. The new tenants would periodically report seeing a man walking along with a lantern in "the acre of stone."

The last sighting occurred in 1948. A bulldozer operator, who was clearing stone from the farm, visited Mrs. Cline's father and expressed his surprise at having seen the old man out walking all alone the previous evening with only a lantern. "You could have seen the field by riding with me on the bulldozer," he said. Mrs. Cline's father just looked up and smiled. He knew the will-o'-the-wisp had been abroad in the land once again.

THE WISP IN THE GRAVEYARD

The legendary ghost arises in the dark, brooding silences of cemeteries. But it wasn't exactly the ghost of legend that appeared to Buffalo County pioneers in the autumn of 1889. It was a fireball that hovered above a grave in the old Indian burial grounds on the shores of Oneida Lake. The size of a large orange, it swayed, like an eerie pendulum, thirty feet above the ground. As the whispered word spread among them curious residents of the area gathered nightly on the lakeshore to watch the swinging light. Occasionally a brave man reached out to catch the light, but it always vanished before his eyes.

A will-o'-the-wisp? Old-timers had a different explanation. They said that a man named Belknap once had recurring dreams in which he saw a crock filled with immense treasures in the old cemetery. He was convinced that if he went there late at night and dug up the crock it would be his.

So vivid were these dreams that finally, one night, Belknap was impelled to action. He set forth with pick and shovel, found the crock, and dug it up. Alas, he had failed to turn around three times as he had been directed in the dream. The minute he bent down to pick up the crock he was stunned by a flash of lightning and the crock vanished.

And since that night the spot has been haunted by the glowing beacon . . . the sign of one man's folly.

THE WISP ON THE ROAD

The will-o'-the-wisp would often form itself into a bluish-colored fireball. It would then hop and skip across the fields. Some say that if a person interfered with the wisp he would become lost. Luckily that didn't happen to Alfred Ulrick, Sr., who had several chilling encounters with the will-o'-the-wisp.

Ulrick was a young man seventy years ago when he first encountered the wisp. The mysterious ball of fire was common in rural Wisconsin in those days. It would appear in an open field near his parents' farm in all manner of weather, rainy or dry, and on the darkest of nights as well as when the moon was full. Farm animals, ironically, seemed unafraid of the object. They would continue to graze even when the wisp was close by in the pasture. But, Ulrick says, no one ever tried to interfere with the will-o'-the-wisp.

The closest Ulrick came to a direct encounter with the will-o'-the-wisp was an incident in July 1909. Ulrick and his father had taken the buggy and a favorite horse named Dick into town for a supply of oats. Their grain hadn't yet been harvested.

Ulrick describes his father, who stood nearly six feet tall and weighed one hundred seventy-five pounds, as a fearless man: "He did not seem to know the meaning of fear, regardless of what the situation was."

On their way home the Ulricks had to travel a road near which the will-o'-the-wisp was known to frolic. Twilight descended on the pair as Dick trotted through the gathering gloom. The night air was cool. A full moon cast a glow across the nightscape. The road stretched out before them "like a white ribbon laid out in the darkness."

Soon, father and son knew they were near the wisp's playground. They began peering into the darkness. A glimpse of the fiery creature would provide ample fuel for a lively tale once they reached home.

And then they saw the will-o'-the-wisp. It was

hovering and pulsating not far away. It appeared to be moving toward them. Ulrick's father reined the horse to a walk for a closer look at the mysterious object. Alfred didn't appreciate his father's curiosity. The young boy didn't say anything, but his stomach was churning.

As the object continued to close the distance Ulrick brought the horse to a stop. In a few seconds, the will-o'-the-wisp was only a few yards from the wagon. That was young Alfred's limit. "I think my body was covered with more goose-pimples than a chicken has feathers; seconds seemed like hours; and I know I stopped breathing."

His father evidently felt the same dread, for he urged the horse onward. They didn't stop until they reached home. Did the will-o'-the-wisp follow them? Neither father nor son ever looked back.

THE HITCHHIKING WISP

Sailors are familiar with a phenomenon called St. Elmo's fire. This round flash of light often appears around ship masts during stormy weather. We know it is an electrical charge, which actually does look like a flame. It is named for St. Elmo, the patron saint of sailors. It is also not unusual for St. Elmo's fire to appear on land around church steeples, airplanes, and other objects when the weather is unsettled.

In early Wisconsin, St. Elmo's fire was often mistaken for the phantomlike will-o'-the-wisp by those who saw it. Such was the case of K. F. Peabody in Star Prairie.

Automobiles were still a rarity on country

roads in the early 1910s, but travelers often ventured out after dark with the aid of strong spotlights. On one particular night Peabody was guiding a horse and rig through a light drizzle. It was late and the road was quite muddy. Suddenly a bright light surrounded the rig. Thinking it was someone coming up from behind, Peabody pulled his rig toward the side of the road and turned to look. Nobody was behind him.

Peabody was startled. Where was the light coming from? Perhaps it was shining on him from somewhere in the dark night sky. He lowered his umbrella. There, on the metal tip, was a bright shimmering flame. Peabody quickly furled the umbrella. The flame jumped to a whip that was held in place next to the wooden buggy seat. As he gazed at the flame he recalled reading about St. Elmo's fire and realized that this must be the explanation. He removed the whip and looked more closely at the flame. It was white, quite brilliant, and similar to the flame of a candle, but it gave off no heat and, in fact, was quite cold.

Peabody returned the whip to its socket and drove on. The flame stayed with him to the top of a ridge. On the downhill side, the flame gradually receded and eventually disappeared when he reached the bottom.

Whether it danced across a meadow, followed pioneers to their doorsteps, or hitched a ride in a buggy, the will-o'-the-wisp was a unique part of the ghost lore of Wisconsin. To the uneducated pioneer, the wisp's appearance was a source of awe and not a little fright. We now know that those lights pulsating over that dank swamp in the dead of night were products of swamp gas . . . don't we?

THE FARMHOUSE "SPOOK"

In the hardscrabble Depression years of the 1930s, when a person's economic security was often determined by luck and resourcefulness, tempers sometimes flared over small injustices, whether real or imagined. At least that's how it was in northern Wisconsin. Roy Nelson,* a bachelor, owned a farm north of Cumberland. He and his neighbor, Elmer Pederson,* had been renting jointly an additional acreage from which they shared the annual crop of hay.

But one day the two had an argument over this arrangement. Soon Roy began complaining about a ghost on his property—a ghost who left barn doors open day and night, filled feed troughs with water, and pounded on the walls of his house. He named Elmer as the culprit. Neighbors, anxious to preserve harmony in the community and to avoid the scandal of a slander suit, didn't dare take sides. They attributed Roy's wild tales to the eccentricities of living alone too long.

But when the disturbances on Roy's farm continued, the neighbors did get involved. After all, Roy was basically a fine man. He always had hot coffee ready for a drop-in visitor, kept his Bible on the kitchen table, and paid his help well. And he was most determined to catch the "billy goat" who was doing him in. Farmers volunteered to take turns, in shifts, hiding out in Roy's woodpiles and watching from the windows of his house.

Roy, meanwhile, carried out his own

surveillance. He ran a wire from house to barn and employed a German shepherd whose leash he looped around this wire. The dog was thus free to run back and forth in hot pursuit of a trespasser. Next, Roy borrowed a .38-caliber revolver from his brother-in-law and stood guard on his porch. Whenever he heard a strange sound, he'd fire into the air, and the shot was heard three quarters of a mile away, above the humming of the telephone wires and the eerie cry of the coyote. Inside, the house watchers, congregated in the kitchen, would hear pounding on the opposite side of the house. If they moved to that side, the pounding was heard on the kitchen side. But with men stationed at both ends of the house, the pounding ceased.

Even children took their turns on the "ghost watch." Art Rasmussen,* a good friend of Roy's, volunteered his son's services for a forty-eight-hour shift. Pete* was twelve years old at the time and says, "I shook from my belly button both ways, but didn't dare say no." He was given a chamber pot and instructed to go upstairs and remain there at all times. Roy carried food and water up to him. A horse blanket with a peephole cut from it had been tacked up over a window. While the boy was watching Roy at work in a field, he suddenly heard a noise downstairs as if someone were pouring water from a jug. But he knew there was no jug down there. "That's when I quit growing," he recalls.

Later that day when Roy returned from the field, he discovered that the mail, which he had picked up at noon, was strewn all over the kitchen. That night someone or something was making a noise with a newspaper and Pete, from his upstairs post, heard Roy yelling at the "billy goat." The pounding on the walls continued as before. Pete says, "After two days of Depression coffee, I went home."

A day or so later the boy was helping Roy with the haying on the rental property and Elmer was haying at the same time. Pete says, "At one time we were all within fifteen feet of one another and the look they exchanged wasn't one of love, hope, or charity."

A short time later, Elmer died, and the ghostly disturbances ceased. Coincidence? Or was Elmer the farmhouse "spook"? If he was, why was he never caught? Was it because no one really wanted to catch him? Because a bit of levity makes bearable the days of quiet desperation? To this day no one knows, for sure, the ghost's identity. Perhaps it never really mattered.

THE RETURN OF UNCLE OTTO

A ghost can make itself known in a number of ways. The poltergeist, or "noisy ghost," lets its presence be felt through a series of rappings, poundings, or other calamitous behavior; the unseen visitor may throw dishes, overturn furniture, clomp up and down stairways, or bang on walls.

The origin of a poltergeist is similar to that of most ghostly creatures. When a person dies, so the experts tell us, an imprint much like a photographic negative is left behind which may take on physical properties and become a force of its own. If that negative behavior is strong, the poltergeist, or in some cases an apparition, manifests itself to onlookers. Thus, we might find ghosts haunting homes to which they had a strong emotional or physical attachment during life. Their imprint, that portion of their being which remains unseen most of the time, exhibits a series of strange events for the current residents of the house.

The ghost of Otto Wolf* in Prescott, Wisconsin, was just that sort of poltergeist. In life, the kindly man, blind since childhood, lived in a rambling, two-story house on Walnut Street with his brother and sister-in-law, Carl and Marian Wolf, and their son, George.

Uncle Otto, as he was known to the family, could hardly have been described as a recluse for he had attended a university and traveled to many parts of the world. But in later years his blindness and frail health limited his activities. Mostly he stayed in his combination bedroom and sitting room on the second floor of the house, rocking back and forth in an ancient family rocker. There he sang German folk ballads he'd learned as a child, and since he was a fine singer the family enjoyed his entertainments.

Carl and Marian had bought the house in 1930, shortly after they married. He was a rather successful businessman, farm owner, and local politician; she was a kind woman who worked as a registered nurse in a local hospital. Uncle Otto lived with the couple from 1932 until his death in 1958, so he had been a part of their lives and the life of the house almost from the beginning.

Two years after Uncle Otto's death, the first in a series of bizarre and often frightening events eventually convinced the Wolf family that the kindly old man's ghost had returned to the family he had loved so much.

George Wolf was a young adult in that summer of 1960 when Uncle Otto first let his presence be known. Late one humid August night, George lay awake listening to the summer night sounds outside his open second-story window. Suddenly, the tree frogs and crickets were joined in their symphony by a new sound. George listened intently. What he heard made the small hairs on the back of his neck prickle. Distinct footfalls of slippered feet paced back and forth over the creaking floorboards in Uncle Otto's bedroom. It was directly next to George's room, and he had grown used to the nocturnal strolls years before when sleep eluded his blind uncle. Yet, it couldn't be . . . or could it? The pace was slow and steady just as it always had been. His curiosity overcame the slight fear cautioning him to beware of things unseen, and he walked lightly down the hall to the closed door of his uncle's old room. He opened the door and was met with silence. Nothing disturbed the quiet of the darkened room.

At breakfast the next morning, George's mother scolded him for pacing around Uncle Otto's room. While George's father didn't hear the footsteps, they had disturbed Mrs. Wolf's sleep in their bedroom directly below. George protested his innocence and insisted that the pacing was not his doing. At least, he thought to himself, he did not imagine the whole episode.

Nearly every night the footfalls would be repeated, only to stop abruptly when George entered the room. He knew that somehow the old man was still in the house. His parents scoffed at the idea of a ghost, but later events would convince them otherwise.

Was George upset at the nocturnal ramblings?

Not at all. Uncle Otto had been a kind, gentle soul during life and George reckoned that his ghost, if indeed that is what it was, meant no harm to the family.

Uncle Otto's room had been left unused since his death. Nothing in the room had been disturbed or changed, including the old cane-bottomed rocker that had been his favorite resting spot. A few months after the pacing was first heard, George was walking down the upstairs hallway and noticed the door to his uncle's room ajar. To his bewilderment the rocker was moving slowly as if someone had just gotten up. Was there a breeze that might have moved the rocker? George checked the windows and doors but could find no significant movement of air—certainly nothing powerful enough to move the rocker—and yet George had seen it rocking. For many nights thereafter George would hear the pacing from the next room during the night, followed by the soft creaking of the rocker. And each time that he entered the room after hearing the movement, the rocker would still be swaying.

Perhaps an errant squirrel or rodent, or one of the Siamese cats in the house, had brushed against the chair while escaping detection. George explored that possibility by scattering white flour around the floor of the room. Maybe he would even catch a ghost or at least find proof of one! His theory collapsed, however, when the footsteps would be heard and the rocker creak but no signs of either beast or man were found in the carpet of flour. Ghosts, of course, leave no footprints.

Why had Uncle Otto returned to his home? Was it out of concern for his family's well-being? There are many cases of poltergeist activity in a home beset by crises of various types. An emotional trauma or sudden tragedy can bring about poltergeists and, in this case, Uncle Otto's appearance was a harbinger of sorrow, as the family soon discovered. A few years after Uncle Otto first walked in the night, Carl Wolf developed arteriosclerosis and diabetes. The diseases would cause his early death in 1970. By the mid-1960s his family was already experiencing hard times as a result of trying to cope with the financial drains of serious illness. As the family faced a double crisis (Mrs. Wolf was told the stiffness she experienced was rheumatoid arthritis), the poltergeist activity increased.

So it was that the winter of 1967–68 was particularly trying for the family members, financially, medically . . . and in the more erratic behavior of their family ghost.

Until that winter, the nightly pacings and swaying rocker had become a part of the family's daily existence. Even George's parents had long ago accepted the unnatural source of the activity.

The ghost knew the family was in trouble. As George Wolf looks back on the events of that winter he thinks Uncle Otto was trying to register his concern over the family's unhappiness.

George had finished college and was looking for a job when he noticed that the pacing was growing in intensity and duration. It could clearly be heard at all times of the day and night, quite unlike earlier years. Even Carl Wolf, nearly an invalid and the last one to accept the presence of the ghost, admitted to his son that he often heard the soft footfalls when he shaved in a bathroom next to the haunted bedroom.

Then, early one morning, George was shaken from his sleep by a pounding that shook the walls of his room. It was as if someone were throwing a giant handball at the wall separating his room from Uncle Otto's. George raced into the adjoining room but found nothing. His parents, too, had heard the booming thuds. Until now the ghost of the old man had been almost gentle in his behavior, but this turn of events put the Wolfs on edge.

In December 1967 the family's financial plight worsened. They were forced into foreclosure and had to sell the house and many of the furnishings to pay debts. The decision was made to move to a smaller house as soon as possible.

Uncle Otto's ghost was not pleased. The poundings and knockings grew in severity, coming now from his old room and minutes later from other parts of the house.

One evening in January 1968 while the family prepared to move, Uncle Otto tried to convince them in a most spectacular way that the house should not be abandoned. George and his parents separately left the house for a few hours, carefully locking the doors on their way out. When George returned later, he found his parents and a neighbor staring at the house. Every light in the house was on and light even streamed through the window of a storage room in which all the electrical fixtures had been removed!

George quickly unlocked the front door and raced up the staircase to the second floor. When he opened the door to the unused room, it was completely dark inside! The Wolfs can't explain the incident except to believe it was a message from Uncle Otto.

On a number of occasions over the years, and particularly during their final winter in the house, the Siamese cats owned by the family exhibited strange behavior near the haunted bedroom. One cat was accidentally left in the room overnight with the door closed. The next morning Mrs. Wolf found the feline standing in the middle of the room with its fur standing on end. Its eyes were wide with fright as if it had seen some frightening scene unfold. That cat never again ventured upstairs.

George also noticed a mysterious cold spot on a rear stairway, which led down to the first floor, and another in Uncle Otto's room. It was, George remembers, like walking into a crypt whenever he passed through those cold spots. He could find no natural cause for the frigid areas.

A few weeks before the family moved, George and his mother witnessed the most terrifying incident in their eight years of living with a ghost. George was in his room reading. It was nearly midnight and the house had been unusually quiet. Suddenly the roar of splintering wood shattered the stillness. George unlocked his bedroom door and quickly looked into the dimly lit hallway. In mute terror he saw the large oak door to the haunted bedroom being pulled slowly from its hinges by unseen hands. Mrs. Wolf had also heard the tearing wood and arrived at the top of the stairs in time to see the door flung into the middle of the hallway. Huge bolts hung limply from the shattered frame. "My God, what's gone wrong?" George asked aloud. His mother didn't answer. They both knew that nothing human could have pulled that door from the wall. The next day George moved into a vacant downstairs bedroom.

Despite the intensity of the poltergeist's recent shenanigans, neither George nor his parents had ever been physically touched by the ghost. That changed a few days after the door was torn away. George awoke to a soft, almost gentle, stroking against his face. It was the feel of a human hand against his cheek, reassuring in its touch. One of the cats perhaps? He threw on the light and saw nothing. In an old chair, however, sat the cat, its back arched rigidly, unmoving except for its eyes, which seemed to follow the progress of something unseen moving across the room. George knew Uncle Otto was saying good-bye.

A few weeks later the Wolf family moved. Although they had loved the kindly old man in life, they didn't ask Uncle Otto along, and he didn't move with them.

For as long as he lives George Wolf will remember that house on Walnut Street and the ghost of Uncle Otto trying mightily to keep the family he loved from leaving the home he occupied . . . even after death.

THE GHOST OF GRANDMA MAMIE

Grandmothers come in all sizes, shapes, and dispositions. But they have one thing in common: they want to be remembered by their families after their deaths. How can they be sure they have not been forgotten? Why not come back to check up? That apparently is what Grandma

Mamie did.

It was a crisp, fall night in 1962 when Pat Orcutt, of Whiting, Wisconsin, curled up in bed with a book. About ten o'clock she happened to glance up from the pages and saw her mother's mother standing beside the bed. Although the woman had died several years before at an advanced age, and was buried in Elmira, New York, her apparition was that of a young woman dressed in the clothing of the 1890s.

Nevertheless, Pat recognized her immediately and recalls that she had a "feeling of warmth and benevolence" as her grandmother's ghost smiled down at her and nodded. Pat called to her husband, but just as he entered the room the ghost vanished. When she told him what she had seen, he insisted that she had been dreaming. They argued about it, then suddenly all the window shades in the room rolled up simultaneously and noisily. Orcutt was uneasy. Then, remembering his wife's relative as a mischievous individual with a colorful personality that was indelibly stamped upon everyone around her, he laughed and said jokingly, "Well, there goes Mamie."

Why had Mamie materialized at that moment? Pat thinks she returned to "see" her first great-grandson, who had been born recently. Pat had had a miscarriage before her grandmother's death that caused Grandmother deep concern. The older woman had cared for her when she was an infant and the family had remained very close through the years. Pat wondered too if the manifestation foretold any happening in the family, but nothing significant was forthcoming . . . at least not for a while.

Then, in 1976, when the Orcutts were living

in Wisconsin Rapids, another strange phenomenon developed. Pat had decorated a wall in the den with family memorabilia, including old wedding licenses and portraits in an assortment of frames. Upon entering the room one day, she found a frame containing pictures of Mamie and her husband and also the paternal grandparents face down on the floor. The glass was not broken and the hanger was still in the plastered wall. No one had been in the house since Pat had seen the picture hanging in place three and a half feet above the floor.

She rehung the picture but several days later found it again face down on the floor. This time the hook had come out of the wall. Replacing it with a larger hook, she rehung the picture.

But the picture and its hanger continued to fall upon the floor. Sometimes Pat found the picture there early in the morning when she came downstairs; at other times, she found it there after coming home from a shopping trip.

Was there a normal explanation? Pat's husband thought the picture either fell from some unidentified vibrations or that the family's cats knocked it down. Could the cats, rubbing against a picture, cause it to fall time after time? If so, why didn't they knock down any of the other nine frames hanging at the same level? One of the Orcutt sons had a different opinion. Shrugging his shoulders, he remarked that probably Grandma had come back because she didn't like being in the same frame with her in-laws. For some time the family joked about this, and then one day the picture stopped falling.

When Pat's parents came to visit, she told them about these episodes, and her mother remarked that

Grandmother, in her later years, had set out to destroy all pictures of herself. She had thrown away every photograph of herself that she could find, and even cut her image out of all the pictures in the family albums. Pat had never known this. Her mother speculated that it was probably the sort of thing a senile person might do.

Was the ghost of Grandma Mamie carrying on this task? Did she really want to remove herself from the family circle? Or was she just up to her old pranks to remind them of her presence?

Pat has no idea. Neither do the other members of the family. They know only that Grandma Mamie hasn't been "heard" from since.

THE PENDANT

Her name was Jan. A pretty girl. Gold-tinged hair framed a cameo face. Her large, gray-green eyes held the sunlight of today and the dreams of tomorrow. She fell in love; she fell out of love. She knew joy and despair. She studied art in college, and during the summers of her young womanhood she loved to swim, to boat, to picnic at her parents' lakeside home near Spooner. Although shy and sensitive, she had the restless, searching mind that longs to know the world, to hold it close. Those who knew her hoped that all good things would come to her.

At twenty-eight she was dead, the loser in a three-year battle against mental illness. Her life had ended at the moment when the doctors said that complete recovery was in sight, when bright tomorrows were within her grasp.

For her parents, Marion and Dick Stresau, and the other children, the tomorrows were filled with the special sadness that attends the death of one who has died too soon.

But that sadness was overshadowed by a series of perplexing incidents that began to occur in the Stresau home—incidents that, in time, changed the lives of every member of the family.

It was Marion who had the first experience. She had been sound asleep on that autumn night in 1967, less than two weeks after her daughter's death, when she was suddenly awakened by something. She glanced at the clock. It was just after three in the morning. Then she felt it—the soft touch upon her arm. Had she been dreaming? She was certain that she hadn't been. Someone's touch had awakened her. Her husband, deep in sleep, lay unmoving beside her. Drifting into sleep again, she felt once more the light touch upon her arm. A spider, perhaps? Insects frequently invade homes built in the deep woods. Although now fully awake, Marion was surprisingly unconcerned. "I felt only a strange sense of peace and relaxation," she recalls, "as I drifted toward sleep again."

Her husband, however, had awakened by now and wanted to know what was troubling her. After she muttered something about a spider, Dick got up and turned on the light. Marion got up also and they threw back the covers and searched the bed, but found nothing.

Many months later, on a trip east, Marion was to learn that her mother had also been awakened at about this same time to see an oval blue mist of cloud float slowly across the end of her bed. The older woman, who had been close to her granddaughter, was convinced that the apparition had been that of Jan. She maintained this belief while, at the same time, rejecting belief in the supernatural.

The morning after Marion's experience, Dick awoke his wife by his restless squirming. "Hey!" he shouted. "There's something moving under my arm!"

He and Marion both leaped out of bed, pulled the bedding, pillows, and mattress off the bed, and examined everything thoroughly. They found no living thing. Dick had been sleeping on his side. Had he had a muscle cramp? Had his arm gone to sleep? No. He was positive that something had been crawling under his arm. Unable to find a logical explanation, they put the matter out of mind and never discussed it again. Marion kept to herself the strange feelings she had that both episodes might have something to do with Jan. Was that possible?

The possibility seemed strengthened a short time later when a friend sent Marion a pamphlet with her sympathy note. Although Marion was not one to be consoled by what she calls "commercialized words of comfort," she admits that she was excited by the author's statement that sometimes the personality of a deceased loved one seems to make contact with the living by the form of a touch. Was Jan really trying to communicate with her parents? Or was Marion merely the victim of "fantasies of a mind recovering from grief," as she wrote in her diary? Neither she nor her husband gave credence to psychic phenomena or superstition of any kind. Yet, there was that persistent feeling. Marion thought it had something to do with the circumstances of Jan's death. There had been the phone call from the mental institution saying that Jan had escaped, that she'd attempted to cross a busy highway and had been hit by a truck. Was it suicide? She'd made previous attempts. Or could it have been an accident? Questions without answers filled Marion's mind.

The week before Christmas, 1967, Marion started to unpack the boxes of tree ornaments. Discovering the tree-top angel that Jan had made many years ago, Marion hesitated. Should she put it on the tree this year or would the memories be too painful? She noticed that the doll's dress was soiled and rumpled and would have to be replaced if the angel were to adorn the tree. Jan would have made a new dress, but now . . . Marion, suddenly overwhelmed by a sense of love and joy, knew that she herself must make the dress. Family Christmas traditions are for tender keeping.

In the morning Marion drove to town and bought the white tulle with silver sparkles that would reflect the tree lights. Back home, she worked all morning, carefully cutting, fitting, and sewing the dress. Just before noon, she stopped to prepare lunch. Suddenly, a flash of blinding white light filled the room. Although nothing like that had ever before happened to Marion, she dismissed it as eyestrain. On her way to the kitchen, the light flashed again. Imagination? Or was the phenomenon somehow connected to Jan? Marion couldn't know.

On the Saturday afternoon before Christmas, thirteen-year-old Steve set out to search the woods for the family's tree. Although he had always gone with his father, Marion decided that this year he was old enough to go by himself. At dusk he returned, dragging a blue spruce with thick clusters of cones. Marion remembers that it was the most beautiful spruce she had ever seen. Steve told his mother an uncanny story. He said he had hiked a long way and couldn't find any suitable tree. Then, when he was ready to give up, the spruce suddenly appeared before him. "Almost like in a dream," he said.

He took the tree into the kitchen to cut off the lower branches. Marion was working at the sink, her back to her son. Suddenly, Steve shouted, "What was that flash of light?"

Marion wheeled around. She had said nothing to anyone about the flashes she had seen, but after Steve described a "very bright, white light," she knew that they had both witnessed the same phenomenon.

That night at dinner Steve told his father about the light and tried to pinpoint its source. Where could it have come from? The drapes were all closed, which eliminated the possibility of an outside source of light reflecting upon something inside the house. No one could explain it.

On Christmas Eve, Steve's sister, Pat, arrived home from college for the holidays. After a long, cold drive, she welcomed the cheerful warmth of the blazing fire on the hearth. She settled into the orange leather swivel chair that her mother usually occupied, and Marion sat on a hassock in front of Pat. The family was engaged in animated conversation, catching up on Pat's news, laughing and talking, when all of a sudden Pat's chair tipped over backward, coming to rest against a window ledge. Pat, with her legs higher than her head, was unable to right herself. Her parents set the chair up, but the chair tipped backward again almost immediately. Pat, bewildered, stammered, "I . . . I didn't do a thing!"

Marion, who had been facing her daughter,

knew that she had made no movement that could have upset the chair. The two women exchanged places and the chair did not move again. If other family members forgot about the incident, Marion did not. There was something inexplicable about the whole thing. The chair had been used for years by boisterous teen-agers and never before had it tipped over.

The next morning, Marion tried an experiment. She found that the only way she could tip the chair back was by bracing her feet against the hassock and pushing. Yet Pat hadn't had her feet on the hassock because her mother had been sitting on it. Again, Marion thought of Jan. Could she somehow have resented the fact that her sister had occupied the chair usually reserved for her mother? And could she have indicated her displeasure in a physical way?

Future events were more puzzling. Several nights after the chair incident, Steve went to spend the night with a friend, leaving his parents and Pat the only ones home. Marion and Dick were sound asleep when Marion was awakened by loud banging on the wall. There was a pause, then the blows began again. The family's dog began barking, but the blows continued intermittently for fifteen or twenty minutes. Marion reasoned that Pat was doing exercises in her room, and she was annoyed by her daughter's lack of consideration. Why didn't Pat quit? Surely she could hear the dog barking. Dick, a sound sleeper, was not awakened by the disturbance.

In the morning Marion spoke to Pat about her exercising at unorthodox hours. A startled Pat replied, "It wasn't me—I haven't done exercises for years. I was sitting up in bed scared to death! I didn't move out of the bed the whole time the banging was going on."

The family searched outside the house. Their home had no shutters or loose siding or doors that might have banged in the wind, nor could they recall any neighboring homes with appurtenances that might have created the sounds. Besides, Marion says, "It had been a deeply cold, still night." There were no footprints or animal tracks in the fresh snow. Could the two women have imagined the noises? Perhaps. And the dog also? Not likely.

Strange events of a Christmas season. Marion pondered them often, and one day she confided in Steve that she too had seen flashes of light. In turn, he told his mother that for some strange reason he had felt a warmth and goodness in the holiday season that he didn't think had anything to do with the gift aspect. Both shared the tenuous thought that the mysterious happenings were somehow related to Jan, that she was trying to reach them, to share once again in the happiness of a special time. The closeness of Jan seemed a reality, and Marion wished she could be sure.

According to Marion's diary, the next strange occurrence is dated February 18, 1968. Pat was at home on her midsemester vacation. She, Steve, and Dick were outdoors on that Sunday afternoon when Marion decided to tidy up the living room. As she reached for the clutter of newspapers on the coffee table, she noticed a clipping—a picture of three young women skating at an indoor rink in Duluth. It had been so carefully torn from the paper that the sides were nearly scissors-straight. She read the girls' names in the caption below the picture but knew none of them. Nor did she know why anyone in her family would be interested in such a picture. Puzzled, she put the clipping aside.

When the three came into the house, Marion asked them about the picture. Pat and her father recalled having seen it when flipping through the paper that morning, but that was all. Had it been torn from their paper? Since the rest of the sheet had already been burned in the fireplace, there was no way to check. Could it have come from someone else's paper? The possibility was remote because the Stresaus had bought their newspaper at the drugstore. Had the clipping been left by someone? No. There had been no guests in the house that day.

The next morning, Marion threw the clipping away but later, on impulse, retrieved it. A few days later, she showed it to a friend who claimed to have some talent in the extrasensory perception field. The friend thought that the meaning of the picture was quite clear. She explained that the three smiling women holding hands were symbolic figures representing Marion, Pat, and Jan. The joining of hands symbolized the closeness and happiness they had always shared. Marion thought the symbolism made sense, but it didn't explain how the picture had been removed from the newspaper.

On the following Sunday, just before noon, Marion and Dick arrived home from a trip to find Steve studying boat-building catalogues and excited about the plans for a particular boat that he hoped to build that summer. Marion was immediately aware of the odor of glycerine and rosewater. As she moved closer to Steve the scent became stronger. The only thing in the house with that scent was a bottle of hand lotion that Jan had left. But what would Steve have been doing with it? Then, as if reading his mother's mind, the boy looked up and said, "What is that awful perfume smell? It's been driving me nuts all morning. Must be some of Pat's stuff."

Steve went off to check and about that time Pat, still in pajamas, came into the room. She said she hadn't opened the bottle of lotion since her mother had given it to her several days previously, and that no one had been in her room. Steve opened a number of bottles on Pat's bureau, and when he found the lotion bottle that had belonged to Jan he identified the smell immediately. But how could the odor have filled the room when no one had opened the bottle? No one knew, but again Marion wondered if Jan were trying to make her presence known. Jan was the only one in the family who had ever used that particular lotion.

In the summer of 1969, the last unexplained manifestation took place. Marion, Dick, and Steve had been talking about a book they had all read and enjoyed and Jan's name came into the conversation. Marion recalls that "there was a happy feeling of closeness among the three of us that evening." When darkness closed in, Steve and his father went into Steve's room and Marion sat reading. The cat was curled on the hassock. Soon Marion noticed that the cat seemed to be staring at something across the room in the partly closed door of the studio/writing room. The cat's pupils were large and black but it didn't act frightened. "I followed her gaze," Marion wrote in her diary, "but could see nothing unusual, not even shadows, as the room was well illuminated."

Suddenly the dog, who had been asleep at

Marion's feet, bounded up and, facing the opposite direction, stared at the glass-paneled door that opened onto the porch. The terrier's tail began wagging and she trotted to the door ready to greet a family member. Marion was startled by the dog's behavior because Tuffy, like many small dogs, was an excellent watchdog, accepting only the family and barking furiously at the approach of any strange human or animal. Yet the two other family members were still in Steve's room; Marion could hear their voices.

Perplexed, she got up, opened the sliding door, and let Tuffy out. The dog circled the area beyond the porch and, finding no one and evidently picking up no scent, bounded back inside. Several minutes later, Marion realized that the studio door was directly in line with the glass door. Whatever the cat had seen in the studio door must have been reflected in the glass door across the room. Could that be? According to ghost lore, animals often have the ability to see discarnate entities that are invisible to humans. Marion concluded that Jan's presence must be in the room and that the animals, recognizing it, were not afraid.

The dog and cat then wandered off and Marion resumed her reading. Suddenly a clattering noise shattered the silence. It was as if something metallic had crashed to the floor, and the noise seemed to have come from the studio doorway. Marion got up and checked the room and both sides of the door. The cat, alarmed by the noise, ran into the studio also and sniffed and pawed around. Marion found nothing that could have explained the commotion.

The touch in the night . . . the brilliant lights

. . . the tipping chair . . . the bangings on the wall . . . the newspaper clipping . . . the aroma of glycerine and rosewater . . . the presence felt only by the animals.

Were these only a series of unconnected events? The imaginings of a sensitive, bereaved family? Or had the ghost of Jan returned to brighten the tomorrows of those she had loved? One classic theory is that the ghost of a person who has died an unexpected death often returns to familiar places. Another theory holds that ghosts of those who do not know how to go on to further spiritual development after death come back to stay with loved ones. Speculation, of course.

But the Stresaus were not content to speculate. They wanted proof of Jan's continuing existence and they found it. The search was long— encouraging at times, disheartening at other times. It began with the reading and study of books in the psychic field and culminated in the family's participation in a prayer group near Chicago. It was from this prayer circle that the Stresaus believe they received irrefutable evidence of Jan's survival after death.

One of the psychics, in a state of semitrance, described a pendant—a teardrop-shaped pendant edged with small seed pearls and filigree work. The pendant's stone was described as being mottled in color. This information was not significant at first. Marion was certain that there was no pendant of that type in the family.

Then, one day about three weeks after the family had returned home, Marion decided that she could no longer postpone sorting through the boxes of Jan's personal effects that had been sent on from the girl's city apartment after she had become ill. Although she had gone through everything earlier in order to send to the hospital the things Jan had wanted, Marion dreaded facing the sad task again—making the difficult decisions as to the final disposition of clothing, letters, jewelry, and other things that Jan had accumulated over the years. But the job had to be done and on a Friday morning Marion started.

In the bottom of a large packing box, she found her daughter's green leather jewel case. The compartmented top tray held an undistinguished jumble of jewelry—pins, loose beads including a collection of baby pearls, and a couple filigreed gold earrings. Marion picked up a round glass bead and was about to toss it into her giveaway pile when she thought she saw something moving inside the bead. She held it up for a closer look and, in doing so, nearly dropped it. The bead was not round at all; it was a teardrop-shaped globe. And something inside was moving indeed. Tiny, iridescent white chips floated in a liquid and, as Marion moved it, the particles changed position, flashing darts of red, aquamarine, and purple-blue. The pointed end of the globe was inserted into a four-pronged silver shaft to which was attached a ring for a chain. A pendant! Yet it wasn't the one the psychic had described; it had no mottled stone.

Marion then laid aside the pendant and resumed her sorting. But, drawn irresistibly to the pendant, she kept glancing over at it. Then she realized that, in looking at it from that particular angle of vision, it did appear to be a mottled stone, the chips motionless in the liquid. But there were no small seed pearls or filigree work that the psychic had "seen." Or? Of course. The pendant, lying in the compartment of the case, had been surrounded by pearls and the filigree must have referred to the gold earrings close by! Deeply moved, Marion sat staring at the jewel in her palm.

The next day at the jeweler's, where she bought a silver chain for the pendant, she learned that the iridescent chips inside the globe were cuttings from a flame opal suspended in glycerine. The jeweler added that she had never before seen a floating opal so large and so beautiful.

It was not until a couple days later that Marion realized the full implications of her discovery. No one in the prayer group, not even the family members, had had any knowledge of the existence of the pendant. Where had this knowledge come from? Only from Jan! Then Marion recalled her entreaty at the close of the prayer circle in which she had said softly, as though her daughter were actually present, "If there could be something that only you know about . . ."

Today the pendant on the silver chain is the family's most cherished possession.

THE PINK HOUSE POLTERGEIST

The hundred-year-old pink mansion sits prominently on Maple Street in River Falls, Wisconsin. The box-shaped dwelling rises to nearly three stories with a roof slanting dramatically upward and a cupola resting like a wooden crown on the peak.

An early Wisconsin lieutenant governor,

Colonel Charles Parker, built the home for his family. Through the decades the house has undergone a number of renovations and uses—apartments, duplex, and single family dwelling. In 1970 Tim and Alice Early bought the house, planning to rent out the second floor and then remodel the downstairs section for themselves. The house had been sectioned into several apartments and sleeping rooms by previous owners.

Shortly after the Early family, which included a young daughter, Jessica, moved into the house a series of odd events led them to believe that there was another occupant in the house—one they could not see.

The presence was friendly enough, according to Tim. Doors opened for no apparent reason, lights would suddenly switch on, their daughter's rubber ball

The Parker Mansion

would inexplicably roll across the room, or a stereo tape player would increase in volume.

"It was just like someone was with us," Tim emphasizes. "You know how someone can sneak up on you and, although you don't hear them or see them, you know that someone is there? Well, it was that kind of an experience."

Only two-year-old Jessica was ever frightened by the antics of their unseen tenant. On at least one occasion the child came running from her bedroom very frightened. She had been playing quietly with her toys, but something scared her. A child's imagination? Perhaps. Neither parent ever discussed the ghost in the child's presence.

A friend of the Earlys, a college student, had rented the room several years before. At that time it was used as a sleeping room. He too had sensed a presence. The student often joked about his "third roommate."

The couple agree that when they started remodeling the first floor in the early fall of 1970 the incidents increased. The two largest rooms on that floor were a living room and dining room separated by French doors. Draperies had also been hung to cover the archway since both areas had once been used as sleeping rooms by previous renters.

"We were remodeling what was going to be our living room," Tim recalls. "We had finished the room. The evening we completed the work I was sitting in the dining room with Jessica. Alice was in the kitchen. And then, at the same time, the light went off in the empty living room and the French doors between the rooms opened. I called Alice and she came out. At about the same time I called her, the screen door on the front porch opened and closed. It wasn't windy at all so we just assumed that our 'friend' had left."

The couple believe the ghost was leaving the house for a very specific reason. Alice thinks it was because they had remodeled the room and were going to make use of it. There was no room for another resident.

Any old house has a varied and sometimes obscure history, making possible explanations for psychic phenomena difficult.

But the Earlys tried to find the source of the mysterious happenings. In 1972, they met a psychic from southern Wisconsin who agreed to hold a seance in the house. Was the poltergeist still in the house? If so, who was it?

The psychic found a "negative presence" in the house, along with the more friendly spirit the Earlys had encountered. Afraid to dwell on the negative spirit, the psychic instead described the man she could "see," a man the Earlys believe could have been Charles Parker, the original owner.

"She saw the porch, which is no longer there," Alice recalls. A house now occupies the area between the long-vanished porch at the side of the house and the street. "She saw a rocker and described Parker sitting on the rocker with a cat in his lap. She said he was very attached to that cat."

The woman psychic also remembers the events clearly. "I couldn't understand why this gentleman was sitting looking out when there's a house there. I just couldn't understand why he was sitting in that chair. And after the seance was over I asked them [the Earlys] about it. They said that's where the road used to be. But I didn't know that. There is definitely a spirit in that house. He's a very friendly one too. I don't think he'd do anything negative. That was his house at one time; he had lived there. Usually when you get spirits that reside in a home, if they're friendly, they were very happy in that house."

And what was the "negative presence"? Neither the psychic nor the Earlys ever found out.

Although they researched the history of the house there was still some doubt that the friendly poltergeist was indeed that of Charles Parker. Their experiences did prompt an interest in psychic phenomena and, whenever possible, they told friends and visitors about their ghost. On one occasion an exchange student from England told the couple the rounded walls in the house were unusual. In England, their visitor said, such construction was designed to keep evil spirits out of the room.

Although Tim and Alice Early no longer live in the mansion, they will never forget their life in their haunted home on Maple Street.

THE LADY IN BROWN

Can some people survive physical death and somehow remain behind, in an altered state, to watch over a home for which they had a strong emotional attachment in life? That question has perplexed ghost hunters for decades. Scores of tales detail nightly visitations to houses by the ghosts of former tenants.

Brenda Weidner knows all about such

appearances. She lived for five years in a haunted house southwest of Durand. Brenda, her husband, Robert, and the couple's two-year-old son moved into a rented, rural, two-story frame home in 1970. There was no indication the house was anything but what it appeared to be—a rather old structure in a grove of elm and oak trees on a country road. It was not unlike thousands of other homes throughout Wisconsin.

Everything seemed normal that first year. Robert Weidner drove each day to a factory where he worked the night shift. Mrs. Weidner stayed home with young Derek. But the idyllic country life was shattered late one evening in the spring of 1971 as Brenda waited for her husband to return home. It was that night when she first heard the pounding in the walls, gently at first, almost too faint to detect. Then the sound grew in intensity. What was it like? "The walls would vibrate and the curtains would shake," Brenda remembers. "I thought at first it was someone outside with a baseball bat. It happened first on one living room wall and then on another wall, and then back and forth. It would go on for five or ten minutes. Just like someone was inside the wall trying to get out." When the hammering ceased, Brenda sat frozen on the couch, afraid to move and reluctant to search outside in the cold, starless, black of night.

The sounds continued periodically over the next several years. The rappings would usually begin after 10 P.M. and continue for several minutes. Were there squirrels chasing across the roof? Small animals trapped in the walls frantically searching for an escape route? Brenda doesn't think so. The sounds were absent during the day and at other times of the night. Robert searched the house and grounds when he returned home that first night but found nothing that could have produced the thumpings. And Robert never heard the sounds on that night or any night thereafter.

Were the noises merely the product of an overly active imagination? Was there an entirely plausible answer? A few months after the pounding in the walls began, Brenda learned she was not the only person to have heard the strange noises.

A local teen-age girl had been employed by the Weidners to watch over Derek when the couple went out of an evening, but the young woman became "unavailable" after only a short while. Brenda and her husband were perplexed.

"We couldn't figure out what happened and I was quite upset by it," Brenda recalls. "I asked her what we had done. And she said nothing . . . it's the house that upset her. She said she couldn't stand the pounding inside the walls; it happened in the living room wall behind the stove and then would move across to the other wall. That's where I heard it, too." Neither Brenda nor her husband had ever mentioned the pounding noises to the girl.

Brenda also discovered that the pounding in the walls was not the only frightening experience the young girl had in the home. "Every time she shut off the basement lights they would go on again and the basement door would open. She could shut off the lights and close the door and go back in there in five minutes and the lights would be on again and the door open. She just couldn't take it any more. She didn't want to tell me, but every time I called she would have excuses. I finally found out why. It was the house."

The baby sitter's chilling encounters and Brenda's earlier experiences proved to be just the first in a series of strange encounters with the unknown.

Young Derek provided the first hint as to an identity for the unseen tenant. The boy's bedroom was adjacent to the living room and only a few feet from the small kitchen. Brenda was preparing lunch one afternoon when she heard her son's voice coming from behind the closed door of his room. The young mother stopped her activity, crossed the living room, and stood outside the bedroom. She heard only her son's muffled voice. The boy would speak a few words, stop, and then continue. Brenda thought at the time the child was carrying on a conversation with someone. But only his voice was audible. For several minutes Brenda listened. At length the boy emerged from the room with a confused expression. "Mommy," he said, "I just talked to an old, old lady in my room." Brenda glanced into the small bedroom and saw no one. She asked him if he were positive it was an old woman. Yes, the child replied, vigorously nodding his head.

He wasn't scared, Brenda says, just bewildered by the experience. She would have dismissed the child's report but for the earlier experiences and her knowledge that Derek had never before made up imaginary people, as do many children. Brenda began to wonder if there was a connection between this mysterious "old woman" and the knockings.

Other events began to take place that reinforced Brenda's belief that some unseen entity was at work in the house. On some occasions she would hear moaning, or groans, whenever she worked in the kitchen area. It would come from behind, but no one was in the house. "It was like someone was in pain," she said.

What was causing the turmoil? Could there be a natural explanation? Or did young Derek actually see someone—or something—in his bedroom? Brenda had never taken seriously the stories of haunted houses or ghosts. But she began to wonder if there wasn't some truth to those tales. Was she experiencing supernatural phenomena?

Determined to learn more about the house and its history, Brenda began questioning neighbors and the present owner of the house, the elderly son of the original owners. Gradually she pieced together the story of Mrs. Gerda Biermann,* the late wife of the house's builder. Her entire life had been spent in the house, and in it she died in the early 1950s. But what startled Brenda were two peculiar facts relating to the woman's last days on earth: Gerda Biermann had died in the room now occupied by young Derek Weidner, and she reportedly had told a housekeeper that she would *never* leave that house! Was it possible that this woman had been Derek's mysterious visitor? And was she responsible for the other mischief in the house?

A few months later, something happened that seemed to indicate that perhaps Gerda's vow was more than the idle ramblings of a dying woman.

Brenda was sitting on the couch in the comfortably furnished living room, watching a television program and waiting for her husband to arrive home. It was now shortly after midnight. She expected him within a few minutes. Suddenly Brenda heard the kitchen door swing open and then close moments later. "Robert, is that you?" she called out. There was no answer. Surprised, she rose quickly and walked into the kitchen. It wasn't Robert . . . the nearly transparent image of a woman wearing a brown dress hovered near the outside door! The specter hung motionless in the air, its vacant eyes staring past the frightened young woman. Brenda gazed at the vision, noting that although the body was perfectly outlined, a vaporous mist seemed to form an aura around the figure. Several inches of space separated the specter's feet from the kitchen floor.

Suddenly the ghost began to move, floating slowly across the room. Within seconds it disappeared into the pantry. Brenda walked cautiously over and peered in. The tiny storage room was vacant. A basement door at the far end of the pantry was locked shut. An overhead light was off. The room was silent and dark.

Brenda was dazed. It was the first time a "physical" presence had presented itself to her. As she turned to walk into the living room, her thoughts raced back to all she had learned of the late Gerda Biermann. Yes, she realized, the specter in the kitchen did fit the description of Mrs. Biermann. The dress was plain and old-fashioned, the face looked haggard and old. Yet Brenda couldn't grasp the possibilities of having just seen a ghost.

She hadn't dreamed the entire episode, she decided, and returned to the kitchen for a glass of water to calm her frayed nerves. But what she beheld didn't help assuage her: the pantry light was now on, the basement door stood wide open, and the basement lights were ablaze! How? Why? She had just checked the pantry minutes before. And yet her eyes didn't lie. She gazed down the rough, wooden basement steps but saw and heard nothing. She switched off the lights and closed the basement door. Now she understood the baby sitter's tale about the basement and its self-propelled lights. What hand had turned them on? What fingers had encircled the basement doorknob and pulled it softly open?

Until the Weidner family moved out of the house, Brenda often found the basement door open and the downstairs lights switched on without reason. Was there a significance in this bizarre routine? Did Gerda Biermann lead Brenda to the basement door for some purpose? Brenda searched the ancient, earthen cellar several times without success. It was old and musty and rather forbidding, but it contained nothing out of the ordinary as far as Brenda could tell.

Other puzzling events occurred. As Brenda recalls, "I had a vase of flowers on the kitchen counter that would move all the time. I'd put it back, but it would move from in front of the radio to beside it. It happened one time when Bob and my son were there. I asked Bob to please quit moving the vase but he said he hadn't touched it. Now, I never saw it move . . . but it was moved!" Perhaps Gerda preferred the vase beside the radio!

The Weidners' dog, a German shepherd, also sensed a ghostly presence in the house. Brenda said that on numerous occasions "the dog would crouch down on her stomach. She was petrified. I knew then that she [Gerda] was around. That dog was absolutely frightened of something."

One particular episode involving the animal stands out in Brenda's mind. One day while she was working in another part of the house, a crash resounded from the kitchen. The dog sprang to its feet and followed Brenda to the source of the disturbance, but Brenda could find nothing broken or out of place. "I never could explain it. I checked everything but there was nothing wrong. Just that loud crash. My dog heard it . . ." and so did Brenda.

Shortly before the Weidners moved from the house in early 1976, Brenda had her final, and in many ways most chilling, encounter with the ghost of Gerda Biermann.

The late woman's son had recently built a new porch onto the rear of the house. Brenda recalls what happened a few days after the porch was completed:

"This was in the winter, about February. I was in the kitchen fixing a meal. My dog was with me and Derek was taking a nap. There was a door which led to the porch from the kitchen which we always kept closed. And then I heard a woman's voice on the porch. But I knew it was empty. I heard her say, 'Look what my son has done to the house. He built this porch.' My dog's ears went up and its fur stood on end and she started to growl. Then the voice outside started talking in what sounded like German. She started rambling and mumbling. I opened the door but the voice stopped. My dog ran out and sniffed at the corners, on the steps, everyplace. Her fur was up. She knew someone had been out there. And I checked the doors and windows and they were all locked from the inside. Snow was on the ground and there were no footprints or tire tracks. But there had been that voice. I heard it with my own ears. That's when I knew for sure it was Gerda Biermann. She was German and I understand she often spoke the language. And the voice had been talking about what *her* son had done to the house. And that was the last I ever heard from her."

The Biermann house still exists, holding any wandering ghosts within its weathered walls. No one else seems to have had the same experiences Brenda witnessed during her five years in the house, and she was the sole target for most of the events. Her husband found the basement lights on and its door open on one occasion but dismissed that episode as coincidence. Derek was too young to remember now his puzzling conversation that afternoon in his bedroom. The baby sitter felt there was something terrifying enough in that house to refuse work there. And the large family dog whimpered and grew frightened on the occasions when Brenda saw or felt Gerda Biermann's ghost in the house.

Was it all imagination? There are far more questions than answers to this puzzle. Brenda Weidner is visibly shaken to this day when she recounts the events of her life in the Biermann house. One thing is certain—she will never forget that old farmhouse on a country road southwest of Durand. It isn't unlike thousands of other houses with one, macabre exception: it has a ghost!

THE LOOKING-GLASS PHANTOM

Joan Lecher was always afraid of the dark and she always slept with the lights on. But in 1967 she moved her family into a house that she claims is haunted, and for the first time in her life she isn't afraid. The ghost provides welcome protection and Joan no longer sleeps with lights blazing in every room. "When I'm alone in this house," she

76

says, "I feel very content and at ease at all times."

The tall white house on the north side of Wisconsin Rapids was built in 1860. It's a sturdy, comfortable place, spacious enough for Joan's six children and the additional "occupant."

The first episode of ghostly manifestations occurred during the Christmas season of 1973. Joan and her former husband were sitting on the couch in the living room. Suddenly, out of the corner of her eye, Joan saw a shadow pass by. It entered the kitchen toward the center of the house. Joan wasn't alarmed at first, but five minutes later a second shadow passed. Her husband saw it too. They got up and went to the kitchen and then into the combination den/laundry room behind the kitchen. They found no one. They checked the doors; they were closed and locked. No one could have entered or left the house. What had they seen? They have no idea.

During this same holiday period, Joan's daughter, Kathy, was standing in the kitchen one day combing her hair in front of a large, old-fashioned mirror. A man's face appeared in the glass. He stood behind her, looking over her shoulder. She spun around but no one was there. She was alone in the room.

Another incident of that time involved a young girl who was living with the Lechers. She was sleeping in the room off the kitchen and awoke suddenly to see a man standing in the doorway watching her. Too frightened to scream, she pulled the covers up over her head and hoped he'd go away.

Both girls described the ghost as an "elderly man," but could supply no details.

Later, in an attempt to make contact with the

apparition, the Lecher children and their friends gathered around the kitchen table for a seance. Someone asked the ghost, if present, to manifest itself in some way. A cup rose up from an open shelf. The visitors fled screaming. On another night, the group heard sounds like the sawing of wood coming from the attic. Joan had begun remodeling the old house. Was the ghost helping? The family never found any evidence of its handiwork.

One night in 1977, Lance, who was eighteen years old at the time, was home alone baby-sitting young Joe. Lance heard footsteps upstairs; someone was striding back and forth in the hallway, through the bedrooms. The doors were locked, the windows all closed, yet Lance was certain that someone, somehow, had broken into the house. When his older brother, twenty-year-old Kim, arrived home, he went upstairs immediately to investigate. No one was there and nothing had been disturbed. And Joe had slept through all the excitement.

But the footsteps persist. Joan often hears them, especially when she is alone in the house. On at least one occasion, the footsteps resounded from a room in which a mattress covered the floor. She says that she is so accustomed to the walking that she no longer investigates. "Somebody's here keeping an eye on me," she says. An unsound business deal and an instance of petty theft in the house resulted in punishment for the offenders and further convinced Joan that a "friendly spirit" is indeed taking care of her.

On a winter's evening, Joan was sitting in the archway between the living room and the kitchen. She faced the large, low-silled living room windows that look out upon the street. In the bottom left-hand corner of one window a light like a flame appeared, a bright, single image that was visible for several seconds. Joan feels that the light came from somewhere inside the house, but no one was with her at the time. Could the light have been a reflection from outside? Joan is certain that it was not; she says that a reflection would have created a double image: one in the outside storm window and one in the inner window. She experimented later with candles and a cigarette lighter and found that both reflected a double image. Also, she says the light she saw was "pure white," not the yellow flame of a candle or a lighter.

Although Joan has never seen the mysterious resident, she feels his presence strongly, especially when she is troubled. The children call the ghost H.B., the initials of the previous owner of the house who was found dead in bed, apparently of a heart attack. H.B. was a bachelor. Has he returned to share in the busy family life he never knew?

The first manifestation involved two shadows. Are there two ghosts? H.B. took care of his invalid mother in the house before she entered a custodial care facility. Could they both have returned to the house they loved to see if the new owners are maintaining the property so that its value won't fall? It's a common occurrence in ghost lore.

Or are the Lechers imagining the phenomena they claim to witness? Children often live in an imaginary world of ghosts and goblins, yet, except for Joe, these children were young adults when the strange events began. As their mother explains, "These experiences we're talking about do not happen to little children. They're already grown people." A group of teen-agers might see or hear what they wished, the collective unconscious mind eager to embrace the supernatural. But what of the recurring footsteps? The face in the mirror? The flame in the window?

Joan can offer no rational explanation. She only hopes one day to learn the identity of her ghost or ghosts. Meanwhile, she is content, feeling "awfully protected" by whoever or whatever is watching over her and her family.

THE PSYCHIC SISTERS

Rachel Harper* and Diane Bonner* are sisters who share a curious talent: the ability to act as a magnet for ghosts!

The first time a ghost visited Rachel Harper was on a Monday night in March 1976. Rachel lay next to her slumbering husband in the bedroom of their small frame home near Neillsville. Her two young children and husband had been asleep for hours. Rachel was still alert, gazing at the darkened ceiling, somewhere between wakefulness and sleep.

Suddenly she felt a presence in the room. A third person was watching her. Rachel looked across the room and saw a male human form pulsating in a foglike haze.

Rachel recognized the figure. His name was Billy—Billy Fulham*—and he'd been dead for nearly ten years! She'd been his high school sweetheart. But, as with many teen-age romances, love withered and the couple went their separate ways—Rachel to marriage and homemaking, and Billy to the army shortly after graduation.

No one knew precisely what happened, but Billy left his army camp one night without permission and was killed in an automobile accident. The young man who had died too soon was buried in the cemetery in the small town where he'd grown to manhood.

Rachel couldn't attend the funeral, but she often thought of Billy during the ensuing years. He had an intense love for the outdoors, and whenever Rachel gazed at a particularly spectacular sunset, or walked across a low hill after a gentle rain, or trod softly in a misty morning fog she remembered Billy and how he would have reveled in these simple pleasures.

All these memories flooded back to her as he floated toward her in that night-shrouded room. Rachel could sense a deep sorrow, almost as if he wanted to be consoled over a great loss. And then Billy vanished as suddenly as he had materialized.

The next morning Rachel told her husband about the strange visit during the night. "It wasn't a dream," Rachel told her disbelieving husband. "Billy was in that room."

Rachel had remembered her dreams before, as many of us do. But Billy was most definitely not the product of fragmented experiences released in the eerie world of dreams.

Her husband scoffed at the incident. Rachel, too, was outwardly jocular over the "ghost." Yet, she was secretly distressed and puzzled by the visit. Rachel wanted to dismiss it as a hallucination or imagination . . . or something.

On the next night, however, Billy came again.

Just as on the previous evening, he was trying to communicate with Rachel. But there was still some barrier between him and Rachel.

"It was as if he couldn't totally communicate," Rachel remembers. "There was this sadness, though, this deep depression. I couldn't understand what he was saying." Rachel also felt that Billy was trying to draw her away; he wanted her to come with him.

For three consecutive nights Billy appeared and tried to make Rachel understand his sense of sorrow.

On the fourth night, Billy came as before. But this time Rachel left with him! There was no conscious movement, Rachel says, no action. She felt herself being lifted by the shoulders and suddenly accelerated to "a different dimension."

Rachel found herself in a place of whiteness and such brilliant light that it seemed as if all the camera lights in the world had been turned on at once.

Where was this place? What was this place? Rachel doesn't know. "It was cold. The beings I saw weren't human and they weren't three-dimensional. But, they had faces, and you recognized them as people but could only see their faces."

Rachel again sensed a suffering, an emptiness in the beings around her; they needed to be released from some indefinable shackles.

The couple passed through this world of silence and moved into a void occupied by a single stone bench with intricate, etched scrollwork on the backrest. There was no talk. No sound at all. Just a pounding silence.

As suddenly as she had entered this realm,

Rachel was back in her home, lying next to her husband. Was it a dream? She still wasn't sure.

By the following day Rachel was afraid for darkness to fall. What was Billy trying to say? Why was he coming to her?

On Friday night, Rachel lay awake wondering if the pattern of the previous evenings would be repeated. She was not to be disappointed. Rachel saw him in the doorway, shimmering and beckoning toward her. He wore the same sorrowful countenance about him. But something was wrong. Rachel knew then that he was saying good-bye. Billy had been unable to reach her. He seemed to want to make her understand that something was wrong.

When Rachel awoke the next morning the episode was imprinted on her mind. She was frightened.

Rachel decided to telephone Billy's mother. It had been years since they'd last spoken to each other, and perhaps Mrs. Fulham* could understand the reason for Billy's visits.

Mrs. Fulham answered after several rings and seemed delighted to hear from Rachel. Casual conversation followed. Rachel asked the woman how she had been.

"Well, all right, under the circumstances," Mrs. Fulham replied.

"What do you mean?"

"Rachel, my husband died last Sunday night."

She froze at the words. So, that was it.

Billy first appeared the night after his father died. That was the sorrow he felt. Somehow, Billy knew that Rachel could tell his mother how sad he was and how much he wanted to be there to comfort his mother . . . but could not.

Rachel tried to tell Mrs. Fulham about Billy but the woman refused to listen. "I don't want to hear about it or talk about such things," Mrs. Fulham said.

But the puzzle had been solved. The final missing piece had been put into place. The visits of the ghost had not been a product of Rachel's imagination.

As the months passed, Rachel gradually eased Billy Fulham from her mind. But she was not able to escape the ghost of Billy Fulham.

It was just past nine-thirty in the evening nearly a year later. Rachel was propped up in bed reading a novel. Suddenly she felt Billy coming down the hallway. Rachel doesn't know *how* she knew, only that she looked up and fully expected to see him standing in her doorway once again.

But he was not there.

"You could just feel him though," Rachel said. "It was like electricity charging through the air."

She spoke out loud and told him that she couldn't go through the same experience again. The ghost never reappeared.

Why had he seemed to return? Or did he? Rachel remembered the stunning revelation by Mrs. Fulham after Billy's first visit.

Rachel reached over to a bedside telephone and dialed Mrs. Fulham. The old woman was in clear distress. "What has happened?" Rachel asked. Earlier in the day, Mrs. Fulham answered, her bank mortgage had been canceled. She had been unable to make the monthly payments and would have to move within thirty days!

Two visits from a dead soldier. And two tragic events in the life of his mother. Coincidence? Or a hand reaching out from the grave trying to console a grief-stricken mother?

Rachel Harper is not the only member of her family to have experienced hauntings.

Diane Bonner, Rachel's younger sister by several years, has encountered three ghosts and seen a vivid dream turn inexplicably into reality.

Diane moved with Rachel and her mother to Chippewa Falls in the summer of 1968. She was a junior in high school and on that particular Sunday night in August looked forward to a new school the next morning. She and her sister were staying with their grandmother until a house could be found to rent.

At ten o'clock that night Diane went to bed. How long she had been asleep she doesn't know. But she was suddenly awake and alert, sitting up in bed. Through an open window stars shone in the distant heavens.

Then she saw the old man.

He was at the foot of the bed surrounded by a vaporous mist. Diane could only see his upper torso but it seemed solid, almost three-dimensional. He wore work trousers and a blue short-sleeved shirt. A full white beard reached to his chest. Diane saw that his white hair was receded to nearly the middle of his head. A bushy moustache curled over his upper lip.

Extraordinary blue eyes gazed at Diane as she sat immobile on the bed. A kind of light seemed to emanate from them.

Nothing was said and the old man did not

move. As quickly as he had come, the ghost vanished.

Diane managed to fall back asleep, but the next day after school she tried to find her mysterious intruder's identity. Diane saw her grandmother conversing with a neighbor. The young girl told the women about her visitor. Her grandmother scoffed at the tale, but the neighbor woman stared at the girl.

"Why, that sounds like old Mr. Banks,*" the neighbor said. "He died in that house twenty years ago!"

Mr. Banks never visited Diane again.

A few years later Diane Bonner had an encounter with a ghost strikingly similar to her sister Rachel's. It was early in 1971, shortly after Diane had graduated from high school. A good friend of hers, Tom Kearsley,* had just been told by a physician that his headaches were the result of an inoperable brain tumor. He apparently had been born with it.

Kearsley was one of the most popular boys in Diane's high school class. He was the type of boy nearly everyone respected and liked, always ready to help his friends without any thought of himself. Selfless was the word used often to describe his outlook on life.

As the youngest child in his family, Tom was particularly close to his parents and especially his father, whom he idolized.

Diane and her boyfriend, whom she would later marry, were the only close friends to whom Tom confided his tragic news. Six months after the tumor was first diagnosed Tom, Diane, and a group of friends attended a party on a Friday night. The next morning Diane learned that Tom had been rushed to a hospital and doctors were preparing to perform emergency brain surgery. Before the operation could begin, Tom Kearsley died.

"I didn't find out about his death until later in the afternoon," Diane said. "But about eleven in the morning I suddenly felt my skin tingle and I immediately thought of Tom. A friend called later and said Tom had died at about ten-thirty that morning."

He was buried the following Tuesday. The next night Diane awoke with a start at about eleven-thirty. She looked across the room and Tom was standing only a few feet away from her bed. He looked as he did in life, as if he had never died.

Diane relates what happened next. "There was no verbal communication between us, but it was almost as if I could read his thoughts. And he said, 'Diane, I know everyone feels bad about my death, but please tell them not to worry. I'm happy here.' And then he left."

It was very difficult for his friends to accept Tom's death. Whenever they would gather the conversation inevitably turned to Tom and how he was missed so very much. Diane accepted his death better than most of his grieving friends and relatives. "He was only nineteen but he had a very good life. People adored him. What more could anyone want?" she would remind them.

Perhaps that is why the ghost of Tom Kearsley came once again to Diane. It was about a week after his burial. Just as before she awoke in the middle of the night to see a vague form of a man standing before her.

"Please tell everyone to leave me alone," the ghost told Diane. "I know everyone is still upset. But, please, have them remember the good times and leave me alone."

Even after life Tom was concerned and moved by friends in distress. Diane carried out his commands, and the ghost was released from his earthly wanderings.

Two years later Diane had her third session with a ghost. By then married, she and her husband were living in a hundred-year-old frame house on Elm Street in Chippewa Falls.

Shortly after the couple moved in, Diane was busying herself with makeup in front of a large mirror in the upstairs bathroom. She reached down for a brush, and when she glanced back into the mirror she saw two reflections! A disembodied head of an old woman was staring at her from somewhere over Diane's shoulder.

The head of the ancient crone was weathered and deeply etched with wrinkles. Her cheeks were sunken and the face had such a total look of emaciation that Diane could barely distinguish the woman's lips and mouth. Long gray hair was pulled tightly back into a bun and parted straight down the middle. The woman seemed to have no eyes, only a leathery face that didn't move or speak.

Diane turned to look behind her but saw only the empty room. When she looked back into the mirror the face had vanished.

She never again encountered the old woman in the mirror, and she never discovered who the ghost might have been.

Diane Bonner's last encounter with the unknown happened upon her father's death in October 1977. Her parents had been divorced in 1960. Diane and

Rachel had always lived with their mother and rarely saw their father.

Diane clearly remembers the "dream" she had the night before she learned of her father's death.

"The dream wasn't about my father, but he kept appearing in it," Diane recalls. "I don't believe I'd dreamed about him since he'd left us."

At the end of the dream, Diane saw herself at a table with a stack of large-denomination bills in front of her. A stranger was beside her. The money was hers, he said. But its source or purpose was not clear.

The next evening Diane's mother called. She had somber news. "Well," Diane replied, "if it has anything to do with money it has to be good news."

Her mother was strangely silent. Then she told her daughter that Diane's father had died the night before. The most unsettling news came next. Diane would receive an inheritance from her father's estate. Depending upon the final settlement, she could receive as much as ten thousand dollars.

How had her mother known about the inheritance so shortly after her former husband's death? Diane learned that her father had discussed his will with his former wife only a few weeks before, but he had made Diane's mother promise to keep the terms of the estate confidential.

In this instance, a dream turned out to be incredibly accurate.

Ordinary Wisconsin sisters with extraordinary experiences. Why have these events happened to Rachel Harper and Diane Bonner? Do they have a peculiar ability to see beyond our world and somehow attract restless spirits from another dimension? There are some who may have that ability. Are Rachel and Diane two of them?

THE DOG MEADOW LIGHTS

Vacationers to the Eagle River area of Wisconsin find peace and relaxation in this northern playground of lakes and woods. But now they're finding something else . . . mysterious lights that linger in the night skies about thirty miles north of Eagle River (five miles north of Watersmeet, Michigan).

Although some local people claim to have seen the strange lights over a long period of time, the first reported sighting was in 1966. A carload of teen-agers had stopped one clear evening along a swampy area of the old Military Road called Dog Meadow. Suddenly a brilliance filled the car's interior and lit the power lines paralleling the road. The frightened young people fled to report their experience to the sheriff. Since that time, many have witnessed the phenomenon, but none can explain it.

Local lore spins haunting legends. Some say that one night, about forty years ago, a railroad switchman, lantern in hand, was crushed to death between two cars while attempting to signal the train's engineer. Others say that an engineer was murdered along the old railroad grade where the lights appear. A third story tells of a mail carrier and his sled dogs who were mysteriously slain a hundred years ago at Dog Meadow. The lights appear near the scenes of these various alleged tragedies and are thought to be connected with them. The lights can be seen on almost every clear night in all seasons of the year.

One motorist, coming up over the crest of the gravel road that runs parallel to the old abandoned track bed, faced a golden bull's eye and, thinking it to be a one-eyed car, pulled off the road to avoid a head-on collision. There was no car.

On a frigid winter evening, a group of snowmobilers came upon the light. Not knowing what to make of it and badly frightened, they tried to surround it, to no avail. It vanished as quickly as it had appeared.

On another night, a drunken fellow from Eagle River shot at the light but it disappeared first. The light is usually the size of a weather balloon, appearing on the northwest horizon and seeming to move toward the northeast.

On a hot June evening in 1977, Elmer Lenz and Harold Nowak of Wisconsin decided to check out the phenomenon. A newspaper account said that no sooner had they parked their car on the gravel road than the light appeared—a bright spotlight shining directly at them. It moved closer, backed away, appeared at an angle from time to time. To Lenz, who grew up in the shadow of a railroad yard, it looked like the headlight of a train.

Suddenly a smaller light appeared below the large light and slightly to the right. Lenz recalled that "the two, at times, seemed to move together, then apart, one or the other disappearing, then showing again." The movements, he reasoned, were those a switchman would make in signaling with a lantern. Sometimes the light changed color from white to red and occasionally a dim green. Lenz judged the lights to be "two or three blocks away."

After watching for an hour, Lenz, still skeptical of any supernatural basis for the phenomenon, determined to catch the pranksters responsible. He and Nowak left the car and began walking. As they approached, the lights seemed to disappear down over the next rise but cast a bright glow in the sky.

A half mile later, finding nothing that might explain the mystery, the pair turned around and the lights reappeared over the rise. When they reached their car, other observers said that, in the men's absence, they'd seen a large red light above a small white one in the middle of the road a block ahead of them. These lights would have been between the men and their car.

Two hours later, the men drove ahead for some distance, parked, and shut off the headlights. The lights reappeared, the large headlight and the smaller one beneath it beaming down the middle of the road. A minute later, the headlight vanished, and the smaller light, Lenz said, "seemed to touch down and burst into three." The outer two lights disappeared, but the third remained, about two hundred feet away. Nowak snapped on the headlights but the light in the road didn't move. Then, several minutes later, it rose slowly to a height of four or five feet and vanished.

Of his experience, Lenz, still perplexed, said, "No teen-agers, no flashlights, no strings attached."

Charlie Gumm disagreed. His search led him to a secluded but well-used side road leading up to a plateau. He suspected that teen-agers manipulated the lights from there. Nightly? In temperatures of twenty degrees below zero? At five o'clock in the morning? It seems unlikely.

Yet, if the light show is not the work of pranksters, what is it? Similar lights along railroad tracks have been observed in other parts of the country, notably at Maco Station near Wilmington, North Carolina. Could they be caused by a luminous gas of some sort? Possibly. Regarding Upper Michigan, some seismologists theorize that the weight of glacial ice in that area has created conditions favorable to future earthquakes, that the earth's crust, compressed eons ago by massive ice sheets, is now trying to expand to its original contour and, in the process, causing luminous gases to escape through faults in the crust. Although anomalous lights are frequently associated with earthquakes, their presence does not necessarily predict quakes. So far, the study of earthquake lights raises many questions but offers few answers.

Meanwhile, curious sightseers throng the Dog Meadow area. They watch the lights. They listen to the legends. And they wonder.

Part II.
Creepy Coulee Country

THE RIDGEWAY PHANTOMS

The year is 1842. Wisconsin is still six years away from statehood. Towering pines blanket the virgin forests, lumbering is an infant industry, and settlers are only now reaching into the remote corners of the wilderness that stretch endlessly across the horizon. The precious element lead has been discovered in the rolling limestone hills of southwestern Wisconsin. For a new nation, still struggling for survival, the soft, bluish-grey substance represents a valuable commodity in the world market; perhaps more importantly, the veins of lead could help produce the bullets and other products with which Americans would tame the rugged land.

The opening of the mines attracted rowdy, tough, dangerous men whose job it was to wrestle the lead from the earth's grasp. From Wales and Ireland, Germany and Cornwall, and the American South miners spread into the lead district surrounding the pioneer outposts of Mineral Point, Dodgeville, Blue Mounds, and countless other small villages. At the height of the mining era, nearly forty thousand pounds of lead would be hauled each year to markets in Milwaukee, Dubuque, Chicago, and Galena.

Roads were cut through the dense forests over which the lead wagons would roll. Alongside the rutted paths another industry grew—saloons and roadhouses catering to the raucous appetites of the miners. These establishments had names like McKillips (near Ridgeway), the Messerschmidt Hotel (five miles west of Dodgeville), and Markey's. There were over twenty-two saloons on the main route, called the Military Ridge Road, between Blue

Mounds and Dodgeville, a distance of only twenty-five miles.

Drunken fist fights, robberies, clubbings, and murder were not uncommon along the Ridge Road. The immigrant miners were joined by various criminal elements, gamblers, and prostitutes to foment a way of life usually short and often fatal. Burial services for the unluckiest victims were informal. The corpse would be dropped unceremoniously into a convenient pit with a few hasty words mumbled over the departed's body.

For over two decades wagons carrying lead for the processing mills rolled down the Ridge Road. The saloons, bawdy houses, and inns thrived. But all that ended in 1857 when the Chicago and Northwestern Railroad completed a branch line into Mineral Point. Lead could be shipped out more easily by rail, and traffic along the Ridge Road declined. The notorious hangouts eventually closed down.

At the height of the mining era, however, wagon masters and wayfarers had more to fear than a chance meeting with a highwayman. Beginning about 1840 a series of bizarre, often puckish, and generally unexplainable encounters with ghosts and phantoms beset those who lived or worked along the Ridge Road. The small community of Ridgeway, halfway between what was then called Pokerville (now Blue Mounds) and Mineral Point, became the center of activities for what has come to be known as the Ridgeway ghost.

The Ridgeway ghost, it must be said, was not *one* spirit but rather a mischievous phantom who could change its appearance at will. The ghost would appear as dogs, horses, pigs, sheep, and several different human forms, including a headless horseman. The ghost roamed the countryside frightening farmers, miners, and travelers alike. It would accompany buggy riders or lead haulers as they ventured out along the Ridge Road after dark, terrify farmers returning from the fields, and generally frighten the wits out of anyone unlucky enough to cross its path.

But is there any basis in fact for an appearance by a ghost haunting the country around Ridgeway? We may never know for a certainty, although there are scores of stories about the ghost and several different versions of how the apparitions began. We must go back more than a century and a quarter, to the early 1840s, to begin the tales of the Ridgeway ghost.

One of the seedier establishments along the Ridge Road was Sampson's Saloon and Hotel. A traveler risked his earthly future in this pit of human scum. The Ridgeway ghost may be the earthbound spirit of one naive wayfarer who stopped at Sampson's.

A peddler checked into Sampson's after a long day's ride, unaware of its unsavory reputation. He was seen entering his room but then vanished. Early the next morning, his fully saddled horse tried to enter the saloon-hotel. The animal failed in its attempts and was soon chased off, never to be seen again.

Soon after the peddler's apparent demise, people began reporting a bizarre apparition on the road near Sampson's. A giant black horse would gallop along the roadway, and on the horse's back was the torso of a headless man mounted backward in the saddle. The headless horseman would keep pace with and often pass the frightened travelers. If anyone tried to converse with the macabre apparition, unearthly groans would issue from the incomplete body.

One buggy driver encountered the headless horseman in a most unusual way. As the driver rode along, he heard the sound of an approaching horse. Turning in the wooden buggy seat, the man beheld a stallion upon which rode a figure in black—minus its head. Instead of passing the buckboard, the horse reared and planted its front quarters firmly in the wagon box. Frightened nearly senseless, the wagon driver whipped his team of horses forward but the horse and rider kept pace. The beast's front legs were still in the wagon only inches behind the driver.

When (or if) the wagoneer reached safety is not recorded.

McKillip's was the name of another, even more notorious, tavern about five miles west of Ridgeway on what is now Highway 18-151. Some accounts of the origin of the Ridgeway ghost stem from a horrifying incident at this saloon in the early 1840s.

Two teen-age brothers, ages fourteen and fifteen, ambled into the establishment one winter day and promptly became the subject of jest by the drunken customers. The ridicule soon turned to murder when one boy was grabbed and thrown into a blazing fireplace. He was burned alive. The other youngster managed to escape out the door but was never seen again. The next spring his frozen corpse was found in a field.

After the boys' murder, a small, gray-haired woman would be seen wandering aimlessly along the road near McKillip's. She would vanish as soon as a stranger approached. Those who saw her speculated that she might be the mother or grandmother of the murdered boys looking for their bodies.

Variations of a female specter abound in the Ridgeway vicinity.

A retired railroad man, Lyle Kramer, told a story passed down by his father. The older Kramer said he often saw two old women on an isolated section of the railroad tracks flagging down a passenger train as it moved along the Ridge Road. When the train stopped to pick up the women, they would float away into the forest.

On another occasion an unidentified man was driving his team of horses along near Ridgeway when he sighted a woman walking in the road directly ahead. She was going in his direction, in the center of the road. He yelled at her to move but she didn't respond or turn. She continued to walk. The horseman drove to the side of the highway to pass, but as he did so the mysterious woman moved to block his approach. He whipped his team into a faster gallop. The woman somehow managed to stay ahead. He reined his team to a halt. And she stopped. After several miles of this frustrating exchange the woman vanished.

Others said an old woman would appear shuffling along the road. She would then disappear into a ball of fire.

McKillip's Saloon also figures into another Ridgeway ghost tale.

A local man was riding home after a visit to the village. As he approached McKillip's he passed a large white oak tree. A sudden gust of cold wind enveloped him. His horse reared, nearly tossing the rider onto the ground. The man managed to hang on as the animal raced wildly all the way home.

The death of the pastor at Ridgeway's Catholic church has prompted another version of the origin of the ghost.

The priest was walking down the steps of the church when he fell and struck his head on the stone steps. He died soon after. For many years, on the anniversary of his death, people claimed blood would appear on the steps of the church and hideous sounds reverberate from within the building.

The church mysteriously burned to the ground several years later.

Whichever version one chooses to believe, there is little doubt that the ghost became the subject of more tales than nearly any other specter in this country. It played no favorites and assumed various disguises to frighten unwary victims. The following stories recount some of the Ridgeway ghost's more infamous appearances.

* * *

The long-vanished Messerschmidt Hotel in Ridgeway was the scene of several hauntings by the ghost.

The hotel's founder, George Messerschmidt, was a member of the county board in 1855. The railroad was to be built from Warren, Illinois, to Mineral Point, and board members had decided to raise the necessary capital by issuing county bonds.

Soon after Messerschmidt decided to sign the bonds, strange creakings and groanings began to be heard in the hotel. Messerschmidt couldn't sleep. Night after night the sound grew in intensity. A voice was even heard echoing through the night, "Don't sign the bonds. Don't sign the bonds."

Perhaps a disgruntled taxpayer had discovered a political use for the Ridgeway ghost! Or perhaps the spirit realized the railroad would take away the traffic along its favorite haunt, the Ridge Road.

Throughout the hotel's history, customers would hear moans coming from the walls and the sound of dragging chains.

* * *

An early Irish settler named Kennedy accumulated quite a sum of money and used part of it to build a large home on some land he owned near the old Porter Grove cheese factory.

One evening he visited the nearly completed house. Kennedy unlocked the front door and strolled through the many rooms. Upon entering the dining room, however, he saw the misty form of a human being seated at the table. The old man fled, never to return. He built a smaller house nearby and lived there the rest of his days, convinced the Ridgeway ghost had taken up residence in his mansion.

Other stories are told about Kennedy. Like many eccentrics, he had a penchant for burying his wealth in the ground. Kennedy deposited his in the earth near the railroad tracks and would check on its safety each day. One night after visiting his cache, he was walking home when he saw a light mysteriously dancing up and down, sometimes dim, at other times quite bright. A train? Or flagman? Perhaps. But Kennedy didn't wait to find out. He fled across the fields.

Kennedy's death was also attributed to the nightly visitations at his earthen bank. As the years passed, his hearing deteriorated. One night a train struck and killed Kennedy as he sat on the tracks. What became of the money? No one knows for sure.

Years later a local character named Rocky Jim Ryan moved into the old Kennedy house. Rocky Jim claimed that at night he could hear the old man's boots tromping through the rooms. Rocky Jim finally moved out the morning after "something" pulled the covers off his bed.

* * *

The Reilly house now stands near a Catholic church in Ridgeway. But, when it was built nearly a century ago, the house was located several miles west of

Abandoned Petra farmhouse

Ridgeway near the railroad tracks. A ghostly history is connected with the house.

An old gentleman named Peavey once lived in the house when it was on its original foundation. After Peavey moved away, the place burned down. Another house was built on the foundation, but the new owners left within a few days. A large black dog would appear, tired and panting, under their dining room table every night after dark. The animal would disappear as suddenly as it had come.

The house was eventually moved to its current location in Ridgeway. The dog never reappeared. Some people think it was the original foundation, or the area in which the house was first located, that caused the canine apparition.

But recent tenants of the Reilly place reported some unusual sounds. When their daughter was young, she would become frightened at a noise like that of children playing with marbles. It came from the attic. The "marbles" would roll across the floor for minutes on end. Nothing was ever found that would explain the incident.

* * *

There are two versions of Evan "Strangler" Lewis's mysterious death.

Lewis was a well-known wrestler of immense size with a fearlessness that matched his physical strength. When he wasn't winning bets in the wrestling rings, he supported his family by farming and helping neighbors butcher stock. It was after a day of butchering on a neighboring farm that Lewis took a fateful walk.

Lewis had been warned not to travel home after dark because of several recent episodes involving the

Ridgeway ghost. Lewis sneered at the reports, citing his strength, agility, and the butcher knives he carried as protection enough against any would-be phantom.

One version of what happened next says Lewis was walking across a field when a white horse with a driverless carriage charged at him. Lewis jumped out of the way and as he did so the horse and carriage rose and disappeared into the sky. He ran all the way home.

The second tale also has Lewis crossing a large pasture. He suddenly felt something warm breathing on his hand. Lewis turned and stared directly into the red eyes of an immense black dog. He tried to chase it away but the beast kept following at a distance. A few yards farther along Lewis again felt the panting beast at his heels. This time he aimed a kick directly at the dog, but his foot flew through empty space where the dog had been only seconds before. It was gone.

Running now, Lewis thought safety was within his grasp. Darkness was now complete as he crashed through the brush. His cabin only a hundred yards away, Lewis again felt the pressure of the black beast at his back. This time Lewis extracted one of the butcher knives and slashed at the dog, hitting nothing but air. He continued to fight off the dog until he was within sight of his house when the canine disappeared.

When Lewis reached home he was dripping with sweat, shaking and exhausted. His family sent for the doctor. Upon examining the still-traumatized Lewis, the physician stated that the man's heart had moved nearly two inches from its original location.

Lewis died on May 8, 1874, two days after his run-in with the phantom dog.

All sorts of strange animals have been sighted as part of the Ridgeway ghost stories. Pigs, sheep, horses, dogs, and "critters" are part of the ghost lore in this corner of Wisconsin.

One night many decades ago, Mr. and Mrs. Buckingham were returning home from a day of shopping. As their buckboard approached Markey's Saloon, two miles west of Ridgeway, Mrs. Buckingham noticed what she thought was an animal in the road. Her husband squinted into the gloom and said it looked like a new breed of dog. Whatever it was, the couple claimed the entire area around the animal was illuminated with sparks flying from its back. The horses nearly bolted at the sight. The apparition slowly vanished. The Buckinghams never discovered the creature's origin.

* * *

Boo Tesch and his dog were returning home about 12:30 A.M. following an evening at a friend's house. As they passed a low bank of earth Tesch heard a sound. Looking at the top of the ridge, Tesch saw a huge, snarling dog crouched as if ready to spring at any moment.

Tesch's dog took one look at the creature and scampered down the road, tail between its legs, whimpering all the way. Tesch was left alone. He looked for something to use as a weapon and found a stone, which he hurled at the grotesque animal. The rock missed its target and the dog was now circling the hapless Tesch. And then, just as suddenly as it had appeared, the dog vanished.

For fifty years after the incident, until his death, Tesch could not rationally explain what he saw or forget that night.

*   *   *

Sailor Dave Jones often courted his future wife at her home in what is now part of Governor Dodge State Park, north of Dodgeville.

Jones was returning home one evening when he heard sheep bleating on the trail behind him. He stopped his horse and a herd of sheep passed on either side of the startled rider. Behind the sheep rode two silent men. They did not look at Jones or say a word. The sheep and their stoic herders faded into the distance.

Soon after the incident, a group of men examined the trail but could find no sign of sheep or the riders.

*   *   *

George Russell, a farmer near Ridgeway, had arranged with another man to purchase a pig. Russell agreed to meet the man in Ridgeway where he would pay cash for the pig. The two met, the pig was transferred into Russell's crate on the back of his wagon, and the seller left. Russell performed a few errands in the village and finally hitched up his team for the drive home.

At his farm, Russell backed the wagon up to the chute and opened the crate, but, instead of the pig, a large dog emerged. To this day no one knows how the exchange took place, whether it was the work of the Ridgeway ghost, or whether a practical joker had some fun at Russell's expense.

*   *   *

Interestingly, one of the phantoms often sighted near Ridgeway was a pig or a drove of pigs.

One particular teamster reported that he

encountered several pigs on the Military Ridge Road. As he approached, they dissolved into a cloud of dust.

* * *

Wagon drivers would often stop at one (or several) of the saloons for "courage," knowing they were within the stamping grounds of the Ridgeway ghost.

John Riley was one of those who stopped regularly at a saloon near Ridgeway. His team of oxen would stand outside with a load of pig lead destined for Galena.

One night after finishing his brew he stepped outside the door and beheld a strange spectacle. His oxen had been rehitched to the rear of the wagon. And walking down the road was the Ridgeway ghost with a whip in one hand and a lantern in the other.

John Riley spent the night in the tavern.

* * *

There is a "haunted grove" west of Ridgeway on Highway 18. During the era when it was known as the Ridge Road a phantom would often appear to startled passers-by.

One story recounts the tale of a man on foot who encountered a team of huge black stallions pulling a black carriage. The apparition charged directly at the immobilized walker and, incredibly, passed directly over the man, leaving him lying prone in the dirt, dazed and frightened.

Other travelers going through the "haunted grove" would report that a strange white apparition flew out at them from the forest before disappearing into the brush. Some heard an eerie, wailing scream from the bowels of the grove. No one ever ventured in to investigate.

*   *   *

One old gentleman didn't believe in the Ridgeway ghost. The fellow took a short cut through the Ridgeway cemetery one evening. A bright light suddenly shone upward from a tombstone and ghastly screams pierced the night air.

From that day forward the elderly man was reportedly afflicted with a nervous disorder.

*   *   *

A young girl was returning home from a visit to a neighboring farm when she saw a light coming from within a barn her family used as a horse stable. Thinking it was her father checking on the animals, she approached the barn but the light suddenly vanished.

Inside, she could find no one. And yet she claimed to have felt a presence. Perhaps the Ridgeway ghost looking for a new horse?

*   *   *

The Ridgeway ghost apparently took various human forms.

A young man named Jim Moore was visiting his sweetheart near Blue Mounds. The young lady lived in a large two-story frame house with an outside stairway leading to the girl's apartment on the top floor. It was dusk when the suitor climbed the steps to the apartment. He paused at the top landing to catch his breath before knocking on the door. From there he looked down and saw an old man perched atop a rusted stove lying in the yard. Moore had never seen the elderly man before and thought there was something strange about him. Moore went inside and told his story about the visitor in the yard. The girl was concerned and, as the night progressed, tried to persuade her beau to spend the night. Moore didn't think it was proper and declined.

Moore left and started home on foot. Suddenly the old gentleman was at his side matching Moore's stride step for step. The vaporous figure did not speak a word and stared straight ahead. As Moore neared his house he heard a small explosion and the old man vanished.

Moore broke into a run and made it safely into his house. As he leaned panting against the kitchen door, he realized the Ridgeway ghost had escorted him home.

Jim Moore never visited that girl again.

* * *

In the era before automobiles, young couples would often walk short distances to visit friends. So it was that near Wakefield a young man and his new bride accepted an invitation to a party at a home a few miles away.

The night came dark and still. The only light blazed from their swinging lanterns, pointing the way through the heavy woods. The air had not yet cooled from an unusually hot day in early autumn. No breeze stirred the air. Freshly fallen leaves formed a dark carpet upon which their footsteps made a faint rustling sound.

Without warning, something stirred in the path a few yards ahead. Thinking it was a neighbor also walking to the party, the young man called out a greeting, but there was no answer. Abruptly the night air turned cold. Their lantern's glow reflected upon leaves fluttering in the air for no apparent reason. The sound of footsteps reached their ears, and looking down they could see the imprints of a man's shoes.

Although they saw nothing, the couple claimed to have felt a presence in the forest. The Ridgeway ghost out for an evening stroll?

*   *   *

Willy Powell passed a pleasant evening with his girlfriend in Ridgeway and was returning home in his buckboard hitched to a fine pair of coal black horses. The winter night was particularly cold with masses of swirling snow drifting across long stretches of the road.

Hurrying the animals along, Powell turned in to the drive which led to the warmth and safety of his cabin. Without warning his horses reared suddenly and the cutter overturned, tossing Powell into a snowbank. As Powell looked up he saw the object of his horses' fright: a towering black figure stood in the doorway of the barn. Powell scrambled to his feet and raced for the cabin to rouse his sleeping brother.

The pair returned to the barn to find the door closed and no signs of an intruder. The horses were not found for several days.

*   *   *

An old man who lived by himself reported that the Ridgeway ghost visited him one night during chores.

The fellow had walked out to the pump to fill several buckets with water. On his way back into the house he turned and saw that the pump handle was still vigorously moving up and down. At once he realized the ghost was getting a drink. The terrified farmer ran into his kitchen and bolted the door.

*   *   *

Country doctors were regularly called out at night to isolated farms to deliver babies or look after the sick. Doc Cutler, who tended the people of Ridgeway for years, took the ghost stories quite seriously.

Cutler would avoid the main Ridge Road if at all possible since the ghost was known to frequent the area. On those occasions when he had to travel the highway, the Ridgeway ghost would always keep him company. The phantom would spring from the brush and perch on one of the doctor's horses or stand on the tongue of his buggy. Cutler tried whipping his horses into a faster gait but the ghost would not be deterred. And, all the while, the ghost would stare up at the frightened physician with its hollow, vacant eyes.

After one late night call Cutler also claimed that he overtook a man walking beside the road. He asked the stranger if he wanted to ride and the man climbed into the doctor's buggy. For the entire journey to Dodgeville, the passenger did not utter a word and gazed directly ahead. He jumped out of the buggy near the edge of town and vanished into the night.

Doc Cutler was convinced that he gave a lift to the Ridgeway ghost.

The ghost, it is said, was particularly attracted to anyone who worked with blood.

* * *

A man was riding home one afternoon in the hills near Ridgeway when he thought he saw movement in a deserted cabin. He dismounted and walked into the ruins. Sitting in a chair was a vague, white, humanlike form the visitor immediately recognized as the Ridgeway ghost. He struck at the phantom with his whip and the ghost vanished.

The next day, the man noticed there were clear impressions of his fingers in the handle of the whip. Fright had placed them there, he realized.

* * *

Johnny Owens, a Welsh miner, was out for an evening stroll on the Ridge Road. Rounding a bend he saw several dark objects swinging from a limb of a tall oak tree. As he approached more closely, the moonlight clearly revealed three human bodies hanging by their necks. Owens ran all the way home.

The next day Owens returned to the spot with three stout friends. There were no bodies hanging in the tree.

* * *

One day in the late 1840s, a lead miner encountered the Ridgeway ghost as he trudged along the road west of Ridgeway.

As the miner walked, the man realized he was being followed. He turned and saw a hazy form some distance behind. The miner said it was the specter of the Ridgeway ghost. He quickened his stride. So did the phantom. Always keeping the same distance behind the frightened miner, the ghost matched the strides step for step. Frightened badly, the miner began to run, and, yes, so did the ghost.

Finally, after several hundred yards, the miner slumped exhausted on a log at the side of the road. The ghost sauntered up and sat down at the other end. For one of the few times in its history the ghost spoke.

"That was some fine running you were doing back there," the spirit said.

"Yes," acknowledged the miner. "And I'm going to be doing some more in a minute." And off he sped with the phantom in pursuit.

What finally happened? It's not recorded.

*   *   *

Late one evening, two men from Blue Mounds were walking along the old Military Ridge Road carrying a long plank on their shoulders. About halfway to their destination, a specter dressed in white sprang from a thicket and landed on the board. Badly frightened, the men began running, still carrying the board and its phantom rider. The ghost stood on the plank snapping a switch over the heads of the scampering men. The two hapless travelers finally collapsed in the road. When they gathered up the nerve to look at the plank lying some distance away, the specter had vanished.

*   *   *

Three men were sitting in a Blue Mounds saloon, nearing the end of a stud poker game. The stakes were high and a considerable sum of money was riding on this final deal. A miner with a full house won the pot. As he reached across the table to gather up the winnings, a man appeared in a vacant seat, grabbed up the cards, and began to deal. The uninvited stranger wore black clothing with a wide-brimmed hat pulled down low over his eyes, obscuring his face.

The cards began flying from the stranger's fingers and seemed to dance across the room before floating down to the table.

The tavernkeeper dove behind his polished bar and hid for the duration of the stranger's visit. The poker players were thoroughly frightened at the card antics and stumbled over each other in their headlong rush for the door.

The money on the table vanished, along with the phantom in black.

When traffic declined on the Ridge Road following the completion of the railroad in 1857, the Ridgeway ghost also became less active. In fact, it is said that the phantom was seen leaving town on the cowcatcher of a freight train passing through Ridgeway. Others claim the ghost died in a fire that consumed nearly all of the Ridgeway business district in 1910.

But there are other, more skeptical believers, who say the ghost has never left.

Jeanie Lewis lives near Wakefield and has collected stories about the ghost for some time. She is not convinced the ghost has truly departed, citing several bizarre experiences that seem to defy explanation.

Shortly after the birth of her first child in 1959, Mrs. Lewis arose at 2 A.M. to give the baby an early feeding. As she sat rocking the child in the darkened living room, Mrs. Lewis heard the kitchen door open. Turning to look, she saw newspapers that had been placed on the freshly waxed floor float through the air. The sound of footsteps echoed in the air, but no one was visible.

Mrs. Lewis ran to the bedroom to rouse her husband. Together they heard the footsteps and the kitchen door slam shut. And then silence. The couple walked cautiously into the kitchen but found nothing disturbed. The newspapers were still arranged neatly on the floor and the damp ground outside the door bore no impressions of footprints.

* * *

This incident could be called The Case Of the Wandering Jacket. Mrs. Lewis says her husband once owned a jacket given him by a former girlfriend. About three years after Mrs. Lewis and her husband married the coat disappeared from a clothes hook in the stairwell where it was always kept. Mr. Lewis insisted that his wife had destroyed it; she just as strenuously denied any involvement. Mrs. Lewis searched the house thoroughly but no sign of the coat could be found.

Several years passed. Then one afternoon as Mrs. Lewis walked down the stairs she saw the coat hung, as always, on the peg. But the garment was nearly in shreds. It was as if someone had worn it nearly every day since its disappearance.

* * *

An old schoolhouse in Wakefield has been converted into a recreation center. Along with the Folklore Village Farm, there is quite a complex for neighborhood youngsters. Some peculiar incidents have taken place there.

At about the time the school was undergoing its face lifting, Jeanie Lewis, who lives within sight of the place, happened to glance toward the sky one evening. On the eastern horizon she noticed a bright, colorful object directly over the Wakefield cheese factory. It hovered over the factory and began to descend. Then it took off to the north and stopped over the old schoolhouse. While Mrs. Lewis watched, the lights appeared to descend into the chimney of the old building.

Several times since that night, children and others visiting the schoolhouse have reported strange sounds from within that chimney. It is said the Ridgeway ghost visits there every so often.

Meanwhile, a bleak, abandoned farmhouse on the old Petra property is said to be the permanent residence of the Ridgeway ghost. It sits surrounded by weeds past the pioneer Ridgeway cemetery south of town and looks just like the sort of place a ghost would inhabit. Doors hang from their hinges, windows are broken—altogether an ideal haunted house!

Was there really a Ridgeway ghost? Or did the Old World settlers bring their superstitious ways to the new land, re-creating in slightly altered form the vampire, banshee, and werewolf? The Ridgeway tales and any truth upon which they might have been built are now lost in the mists of time. We will never know for sure, but the legends will live as long as there are listeners willing to believe.

CASSANDRA

Not all family ghosts are kept in the closet. B. T. Jutes* of Crawford County has the live-in kind, a friendly, solicitous ghost who watches over the children and helps B. T. with her genealogical research.

Her name is Cassandra and she first appeared on the bedroom wall on a frosty January night in 1971. She wore a swirling-skirted red outfit and, with her bearded companion, stood before an open, horse-drawn carriage. Her black hair was parted straight down the middle and pulled back tightly over her ears; dark eyes twinkled above the veil that concealed the lower part of her face. Suddenly she dropped the veil, stepped into the carriage with her partner, and vanished.

Only B.T. had seen her. Was it a dream? "I kept thinking I was dreaming," she said, "but yet I knew I was awake. My husband was snoring all the while this was going on. I was awake and I was frightened."

She got up, checked the children, went to the basement, then walked through the entire house. Still uneasy, she went back to bed but did not sleep well.

The next night the carriage and its occupants returned to the wall, this time in black and white, not colors. The woman lowered her veil and smiled.

When B.T. told this story at a seance a short time later, participants warned her that the spectral woman, because of the veil she wore, was a "negative spirit," not to be trusted. To protect her family, B.T. was instructed to mentally put a red circle of truth, or light, around the house, around her husband, and around each of the children, and to keep it there at all times.

Arriving home after midnight, B.T. felt somebody right behind her. "I was scared to death," she recalled. "I wanted to leave all the lights on. And I got going on this red circle thing, but I knew I wasn't keeping anybody out because they were already in, and sure enough—she was standing in the hallway. She looked exactly like she had looked on the wall, just like a real person except that I could see right through her. And she said, 'Why are you so afraid of me?'"

The specter said she was B.T.'s great-great-great-grandmother, Cassandra, that she had lived in Virginia and Maryland 150 years ago. Evil spirit? Hardly. She promised to guide and protect the family. And she also promised not to reveal herself to other family members until they were ready for her.

Later that day B.T. told her husband and children about their guest from the antebellum South. None are yet able to see her, but Danny*, who was four years old at the time, feels her presence and is unperturbed. "I know she's here to help me," he said. The dogs the family once owned also felt the presence but were distressed by it, whining and refusing to enter a room occupied by the ghost.

Cassandra immediately took over her duties as an "invisible baby sitter," even tucking the children back into bed at night whenever they had fallen out. One morning Danny awoke in his top bunk bed with his back bruised and cut. The ladder was on the floor and there was a fresh chip in the bedroom wall that his mother said was made by the force of the falling ladder. The parents had not put their son back into bed, and Danny had no recollection of the incident.

On a hot summer day in 1976 when Danny was nine, he nearly drowned in the local swimming pool. B.T. asked for Cassandra's help in saving her son's life and believes she received it. Although doctors had given the parents no hope, the boy survived.

When the family ghost first arrived, B.T. had already spent ten years in genealogical research and was unable to locate several branches of the family. Birth certificates had not been kept, marriage certificates were seldom available, and there is no family Bible. B.T. said Cassandra supplied the missing links, giving her original information that she was later able to verify.

Was this the reason for the ghost's appearance far from home territory? Ghosts have been reported to leave familiar surroundings and travel great distances to bring information or to intervene in a crisis.

The phantom disclosed her maiden name and the date and place of her marriage. B.T. said, "I wrote to that county in Ohio and I have her wedding certificate. When I gave a photocopy of the certificate to my grandmother, she was flabbergasted because she did not know this woman's maiden name, and she said, 'They were never in that place in Ohio, honey. They were in Cuyahoga County near Cleveland.' They were in Coshocton and they were married in Jefferson."

After Cassandra supplied the names and birthdates of all her children, B.T. went directly to census records "to see if that was my imagination that was telling me that or she was. And, by golly, those names showed up on that stuff!" She explained that her grandmother had none of this information, recalling only that there had been several boys and maybe one girl. There were two daughters and many sons.

Sometimes names and complete addresses of living relatives come to B.T. "out of a clear blue sky—people that I had no inkling they have any connection with us. I don't even look up the addresses. I just write."

Papers that B.T. can't locate in her filing cabinet appear suddenly on top of her typewriter, ready for her attention. "How do they get out?" she asks.

By some nonphysical means, B.T. believes she has visited Cassandra's home twice. Each visit represents an instantaneous transition of environment. "I disappear and I am there," she said. She has talked with Cassandra in the latter's sitting room and seen the daughter, Mary Jane, who was later killed by a horse. She said that when she is in

Cassandra's home, the scene is in sharp focus, but that when she sees the ghost in her own home "everything is in a haze."

Can the mind leave the body and describe people and places that the physical body has never visited? Some parapsychologists think so.

When seances are held in the Jutes home, the ghost watches from a corner of the room, her face visible to B.T., the rest of her veiled in mist. B.T. thinks Cassandra is in the house most of the time, that maybe she was there long before she appeared on the wall. She spends a lot of time by the front door, watching the children come and go; and she is upstairs when B.T. is cleaning there to tell her the phone is ringing or someone is at the door.

To B.T., Cassandra has become a very real and loving presence, "picking me up, or giving me a push to do more."

Is she fantasizing? Did the children, in their sleep, climb back into bed unaided? Does their mother absentmindedly remove papers from her files? Would Danny have survived his accident without the ghost's intercession? All are possibilities.

But where does the genealogical information come from? Lucky hunches? Or words from the past spoken by the specter of a gentle southern lady?

Arthur, The Resident Ghost

Shortly after A. J. Nielsen moved into the house in Sparta, she wished she had not. She was to recall many times the hesitation on the part of the elderly woman owner who had paused, as if waiting for permission from some unseen person, before agreeing to the sale. Yet, from the time she had first seen the place, A.J. had been irresistibly drawn to it. There was a certain charm in the large, airy rooms of a house that, although unoccupied for fifteen years, had been well tended.

But after A.J. and her children were settled, the troubles began. Uneasy sensations at first. Then scratching noises that the family attributed to mice or bats in the attic, except that searches never revealed any evidence of animals.

One night, A.J. arrived home from work at ten o'clock. Upon opening the door, she found her son and daughter armed with baseball bats, their faces filled with fright. They said they had been watching television when they heard someone or something jumping up and down in the attic. Their mother heard the commotion now too—heavy footsteps pounding back and forth across the attic floor. The chandelier in the dining room, which was directly under the attic, was swinging back and forth, and a definite chill pervaded the downstairs rooms.

With flashlights and ball bats in hands, the three mounted the stairs. "The chill was terrible upstairs," A. J. remembers, "and we held our breath as we opened the attic door." Stacks of boxes and records were exactly where they had been placed earlier. Nothing had fallen. Nothing had been disturbed . . . but not for long.

Things put down on a table one minute were missing the next. Doors that were locked would be opened by some invisible means; doors left open would suddenly slam shut. "Always when I was in the bathtub," A.J. recalls, "there would be doors slamming and footsteps all over the house."

Soon every family member was awakened

during the night by either the scratching noises or loud, thumping sounds. Many times A.J.'s son bounded downstairs to report that some presence at the top of the stairs had been icily staring at him. His sister, watching television one night, felt her brother's presence on the stairway. Expecting him to pop out and play a joke on her, she flung open the door to the stairs. There was no one, only a blast of cold air and then a hissing sound that emitted spitballs of light. The girl ran upstairs and found her brother fast asleep.

One morning, the daughter, who occupied the bedroom next to the attic, was awakened by the pressure of a hand on her side. She turned over, but found no one in the room—only a chill. "This was the last straw for her," A.J. says. "She got her own apartment and moved out."

The Nielsen cat was also terrorized by unseen forces. If she were sleeping in the basement, she would suddenly fly up to the main floor with her hair standing on end. If she were asleep in the front room and the chill descended, she would start running wildly. When family members were no longer able to calm their pet, they had her put to sleep.

Because of the nightly commotions and the sudden, unpredictable chills in the house, A.J. hesitated to invite friends over. Two friends, however, did drop in one day and later told their hostess that they had felt a presence. When A.J. had the house rewired, the electrician refused to work there unless she were home. He told her later that he had felt someone breathing down his neck, watching him while he worked.

One afternoon, A.J.'s former husband came to visit his son. The boy had not yet returned from school, and his mother left the house to do an errand. When she got back, the father, pale and shaken, was standing outside the house. "I don't know what happened," he said, "but something made me get out and it's just like ice in there."

On a day when the noises seemed unceasing, A.J. began to doubt her sanity. Going into the bone-chilling attic, she slipped, sobbing, to the floor. Suddenly a strange calm filled the room, and she began to speak aloud, as if the unseen tormentor, whatever it was, could hear her. "Why are you doing this to me?" she remembers saying. "I have never hurt you and I have no other place to go."

Then she felt the pressure of a hand on her shoulder, a reassuring hand that seemed to convey warmth and understanding. A.J. felt that some kind of truce had been reached. The noises did subside after that, and then one day the presence materialized. A.J. describes him as "a slight man in a dark suit and a white shirt. The pantlegs were narrow like they wore years ago." A large orange cat was at the specter's side. Both appeared faintly, as if wrapped in mist. Was the cat responsible for the scratching noises? A.J. wondered.

In the days to come, A.J. caught glimpses of her resident ghost standing looking out a window or going quietly upstairs. Gradually, she began to hold one-sided conversations with him. She called him Arthur and thought he seemed pleased. Occasionally, she even asked him to watch the house while she was gone.

Once Arthur took a trip for a few days but left the cat behind. "He'd rub against my legs when I was cooking at the stove," A.J. recalls, "and when I'd look down I'd see his shadowy figure just disappearing." Sometimes she would hear the cat jump to the floor and notice the flutter of the window curtains, as if the animal had been sitting in the sill. Then Arthur returned. His human companion knew he was back because she heard the locked door slam shut. Checking the door, she found it still locked. She watched him go upstairs, carrying an old-fashioned valise with strap bindings.

Although A.J. had begun looking for another place to live, she continued to fix up her present home, and Arthur, approving of the work, became increasingly helpful and protective toward her. One day, while painting, she slipped on the stepladder. Unseen hands caught her and lifted her to safety. Another day, late for work and unable to find her car keys, she asked Arthur for help. Suddenly she heard a thud and the keys appeared on the table. She thanked her helper and left.

When an unexpected bill arrived in the mail, A.J. worried about how to pay it . . . but not for long. The sudden pressure of a hand on her arm guided her to the drawer where she kept tablecloths. There, under the linen, was the money she needed.

After her watch broke, A.J. claims that Arthur guided her to the attic where she found a small gold watch in the middle of the floor. In all her trips to the attic she had never seen it, nor had her son. She was certain it had not been there before. She took the watch to a jeweler who said that although it had not run for a long time it needed only cleaning. The short watchband could only have fit a woman with a tiny wrist. Who had owned it? Could it have belonged to someone important to Arthur? Was this why he was here, waiting for a loved one to return? And was it because of his presence that the previous owners had never lived in the house? A.J. longed to find the answers, but whenever she tried to question the former owners she received only strange looks. She probed no further. After all, she reasoned, if word got out that peculiar events were occurring in the house, who would buy it? So she kept the questions to herself, questions without answers.

In scrubbing the kitchen cupboards one day, A.J. discovered a key. Puzzled as to the lock it might fit, she slipped it on her key ring for safekeeping.

With the passing weeks, Arthur appeared more frequently. He often sat on the kitchen stool when the homeowner was baking or washing dishes. But amiable though he seemed, his pranks notwithstanding, he still resented A.J.'s friends. When they were in the house, the chandeliers swayed and an icy chill filled the room.

After A.J. realized that she was becoming "almost fond of Arthur," she worried that he might not let her leave the house, that he might in some way prevent her moving out. But she knew she had to leave. She yearned for a normal lifestyle, especially for her son, whom she felt Arthur resented.

Finally she found a suitable new house, bought it from the builder, and moved in immediately. She claims that, to her astonishment, the key she had found fit the lock on the door of her new house. She says she had never believed in psychic phenomena, yet she has the watch and the key. Where did they come from? Had they been left by a previous resident? A.J. thinks not.

During the months before the old place sold, it remained vacant of human occupants, and A.J. made regular trips back to air it out and clean it. "I could still feel the presence," she remembers, "but he was much quieter than usual, almost a little sad." He was also becoming less visible.

Eventually the house did sell. When A.J. left it for the last time, two little girls were playing outside. "Look," they said, "there's a man in your upstairs window."

A.J. looked up and whispered, "Good-bye, Arthur." He raised his hand in a farewell and vanished. His cat remained in the window a moment longer, then it too was gone.

Part III.
Wisconsin Valley Specters

Haunted Inns

What is it about old wayside inns that stirs visions of ghostly inhabitants? Is it that so much life—and death—have passed through their portals? Perhaps the very transience of the guests invites speculation about their purposes. The signboard above the oak door rocks in the wind on a blustery night, all the while announcing food and lodging for the weary traveler. The implied offer of geniality and warmth was a welcome respite from the harshness of hours on horseback or a swaying stagecoach during pioneer days. But with so much life crammed under a single roof, the geniality often turned to violence.

Several early Wisconsin hostelries developed seedy reputations based upon their rough clientele. Later some of these inns came to be known for their, shall we say, unnatural occupants. What evil was done in those long-forgotten waysides to provide the stuff of which legends and ghost stories are made?

THE GRINNING SKELETON

An early Wisconsin settler called Brechler encountered one such unfriendly specter when he had the misfortune to spend several evenings in a town never recorded. His family was in New York State waiting for him to find a homestead. After a long search, Brechler found his future farm site and set about to find temporary accommodations in a village close by.

Much to his chagrin, a badly weathered, run-down inn was the only available lodging. It was hardly the type of dwelling to which he was accustomed, but at least there was a roof and the room was cheap. Tomorrow he would find something better.

The man was tired after his long search and went directly to his room. A bed, washstand, and ancient bookcase filled with musty volumes were the sparse furnishings. Brechler hardly noticed, falling asleep before the sun departed the horizon.

The night was only half gone when Brechler awoke with a start, sensing more than seeing a movement in the shadowy room. He lay perfectly still, not sure if his alarm had not been triggered by a dream. He turned to look. The moonlight filtering in through a dusty, uncurtained window fell upon the cloaked figure of an old woman huddled near the bookcase. Silently and methodically she was taking books from the case and placing them on the floor. When the shelves were empty she reversed the process until once again the bookcase was full. Then she vanished.

Brechler lay in bed puzzled and distressed by his bizarre night caller. Who was she? What was she searching for in the bookcase? He had no answers and resolved that after breakfast the next morning he would quiz some of the townspeople about the ghostly woman in gray.

Later that morning, Brechler found an old man willing to talk about the phantom. Yes, there was such a thing, the old codger admitted. But he warned Brechler not to speak to it. Terrible things had happened to previous occupants of the room when they tried to question the woman.

Brechler searched the town for other accommodations but could find nothing. At sundown he nervously retreated to his room. He went to sleep without trouble. As on the previous night, he awoke several hours later to a faint rustling near the bookcase. She was back again, hunched over the bookcase, performing the same bizarre ritual with the books.

By this time Brechler was wide awake and determined to identify the intruder. Propping himself on the feather pillow, Brechler yelled at the figure, demanding to know who she was.

Without answering, the woman stopped her book browsing and turned slowly toward the startled homesteader. She glided silently toward the bed. As she neared, Brechler drew back in horror. He was staring not into the face of a woman but rather the chilling countenance of a skeleton garbed in a gray cloak. Two gaping black holes rested where its eyes should have been, and an unearthly grin spread across its ashen skull. The form bent slowly over the quivering man and raised its bony hands. The wraith's thumbs came down upon Brechler's head and pushed him deep into the mattress and unconsciousness. When he regained his senses the apparition was gone. His head burned and ached as if a log had been dropped on his skull.

It is said that Brechler carried the marks on his forehead made by that grinning skeleton until the day he died.

THE GALLOPING GHOST OF MERRIMAC

Peace officers were scarce on the early Wisconsin frontier. The only law was often that which pioneers established among themselves. Justice was meted out swiftly to those transgressors unfortunate enough to be captured.

So it was that the Ferry House Inn at Merrimac came to be associated with a "galloping ghost" during the last century.

Reports from those who saw the mounted specter believe it was in some way connected with a bloody crime committed at the inn, although no such incident has been attributed to the Ferry House.

The grim visage would race along the road near the inn astride a coal black stallion. Victim . . . or perpetrator? We will never know.

THE GUESTS WHO REMAINED

Strangers passing through Hale's Corners on the Janesville plank road a hundred years ago often spent the night at the Layton House Inn. The hotel was built in 1844 by the founder of Milwaukee's old Layton Art Gallery.

The brick structure fell into decay many years ago and was eventually incorporated into another building, which still stands. During the days the inn sat idle, forgotten by all but a few old-timers, passers-by would often report strange sounds from within the empty, decrepit hotel, almost as if the inn had never closed.

Perhaps some guests never did leave.

THE INTRUDER

Ethel Van Patten was a young girl of eight when her parents bought the large sixty-year-old Evansville

House in 1894 for a boardinghouse. The former hotel had innumerable rooms, halls, and musty corners, which the curious child reveled in exploring. An old barn, once used as a livery stable, held a glimpse of pioneer life with its hand-hewn log rafters and windowsills. On the veranda, which stretched halfway around the house, little Ethel would sit for hours listening to the legends and mysteries connected with the ancient structure. But one particular story came startlingly to life.

As Ethel was told the tale by an eccentric Scottish boarder, Patrick McGlinn, the Evansville House once served as a stagecoach stop on the road between Madison and points southward. A number of servants were employed to look after the guests, cook meals, clean the rooms, and generally attend to the numerous chores connected with the bustling inn.

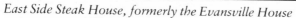

East Side Steak House, formerly the Evansville House

A certain chambermaid, young and lovely, had the misfortune to fall in love with a married salesman who stopped frequently at the inn during his travels. The liaison continued for several months until the suitor, despairing of his inability to marry his love and the futility of his double life, and not wanting his sweetheart to marry another, strangled his mistress late one night. The man escaped from the inn and ran to board a passing freight train. But he fell under the passing cars and was crushed to death.

Ethel was thrilled at the tale. To an impressionable child the story was as good as any that might be found in a dime novel.

Mr. and Mrs. Van Patten also heard the story, but as good, skeptical Yankees, they placed little credence in the account. They had far more earthly concerns in running the boardinghouse.

But late one winter night the phantom walker was first heard. The footfalls descended a staircase near the bedroom of the Van Pattens. They described the sound as that of someone wearing boots walking down the steps. Night after night the footsteps would echo through the quiet halls at about 3 A.M. Yet every time Van Patten would rise to investigate the sound the footsteps would cease their nocturnal sojourn.

At first the family suspected the Scotsman, McGlinn. He was a former sea captain and habitually wore heavy brogans. He was Ethel's favorite spinner of tall tales, but her parents did not share the girl's love for the old man. Despite the charming spell he cast over Ethel and her friends, his language was "earthy" and his influence on the child was not thought to be the best.

Van Patten confronted McGlinn with the charge of perpetrating the phantom footsteps, but, in his rich brogue and direct vocabulary, McGlinn steadfastly denied that he was the culprit. Shortly thereafter his innocence seemed to be proven in a final, still unexplained episode.

All that winter the family heard the footsteps. Their pattern never changed. One night Mr. and Mrs. Van Patten settled down in bed and listened for their mysterious intruder, determined that on this occasion they would catch McGlinn and put an end to his meanderings. Just before dawn they heard the footfalls . . . down the stairs . . . into an office on the first floor . . . and finally the sound of the locked outer door opening and closing. Van Patten sprang from his bed and raced down the stairs. The outer door was still bolted from the inside! He unhitched the latch and stared down at the snow cover on the ground beyond the threshold. There were no visible footprints. No one had passed through that doorway.

Still believing the "phantom" was McGlinn, Van Patten scurried back up the stairs and threw open the door to the Scot's room. In a bed near the wall lay McGlinn, sleeping soundly in his nightshirt and snoring quite loudly.

The mysterious intruder never returned to the Evansville House after that night.

Mrs. Verne Worthing of Evansville said her parents bought the boardinghouse from the Van Pattens in 1902. Over the forty-five years they owned the house, Mrs. Worthing's parents were never troubled by the phantom walker. In fact, they were never told the story!

The Evansville House is now the East Side

Steak House.

Who—or what—produced those echoing footfalls? Was it really Patrick McGlinn adding some "life" to one of his tall tales? Or was it perhaps the restless ghost of that disconsolate suitor who long ago killed his young love and now returned to claim her?

THE GHOSTLY LANDLORDS

The Wisconsin Dells is perhaps the state's most popular vacation area. Tourists by the thousands migrate each summer to this spectacular land of towering bluffs and deep ravines sculpted over the millenia by the Wisconsin River. The modern visitor enjoys the Indian pageants, water ski shows, boat rides, novelty shops, campgrounds, and other twentieth century charms. But all these would pale beside the "attractions" of the Dell House, which stood a century ago near the Narrows in a glen close by a sandy beach and fresh water spring.

When the Dell House was built in 1837 by a man named Allen, its primary temptations were those of the flesh. The rough rivermen drank the bad whiskey, gambled away their meager earnings, sang the bawdy songs, and sampled the delights of the frontier ladies who frequented the inn. More often than not, violence capped an evening's festivities. The churning brown river claimed the earthly remains of not a few luckless murder victims.

The days of the raftsmen passed and the Dell House lost its reason for being. By the end of the last century the hostelry was abandoned. Its hulk was mute testimony to an earlier, vanished way of life. Adventurous tourists and local residents would camp in the glen and thus began the stories of eerie apparitions in the decaying ruins.

By daylight the old Dell House had what one early resident of Wisconsin Dells described as "an indescribable charm of romantic interest." But at night the violent and bloody history of the inn prompted many witnesses to swear that ghosts and mysterious sounds emanated from within the pioneer relic. Campers spread sinister tales of loud cursing, insane laughter, the sound of crashing crockery, and vague, fleeting figures in the moonlight.

The bizarre legacy of the Dell House ended in a fire that burned the inn to the ground late one night in 1910. The towering brick chimney and fireplace, which once warmed the rowdy rivermen, remained for many years until it too was devoured by the forest.

The glen near the Narrows remains, though the Dell House has vanished. Tourists in sightseeing boats pass the spot each summer day. And, as twilight descends, it is not difficult to look toward that glen and see visions of rivermen past, acting out their grisly scenarios all over again.

THE HORSE OF DEATH

How do we learn of death? A relative's letter, yes. The newspaper obituary column, of course. But other, more bizarre messages from beyond the grave have been recorded by man from the earliest centuries.

The ghastly routine of the angel of death has been the subject of many lively stories. None is more bizarre than the legend of the Devil's Hitching Post.

Years ago, a large stone near the Wisconsin Dells, now called Elephant Rock, had the eerie name of the Devil's Hitching Post. Whenever a death occurred in the area, a man riding a coal black stallion would stop at the Hitching Post and tether the animal. The stranger would then stride across the hills to the doorstep of the deceased. The dead man and his unearthly guide would then depart.

Did anyone every actually see the black stallion and his rider? Yes, but the witness did not live long.

The story is told of a traveler passing by the Post who noticed the horse tied nearby. He had never seen a more magnificent beast and decided to go up to the animal for a closer inspection. But as he drew near, the horse's master suddenly appeared on a nearby bluff. The horse reared and his lethal hooves struck the traveler, killing him instantly.

Whether it is a vague feeling of doom, a ghostly visitor in the dark of night . . . or a phantom black stallion, we can be warned in a number of strange ways that the messenger of death is near.

THE WAILING GHOST OF MADISON'S JAIL

On the night of November 29, 1873, Sheriff Van Wie, kerosene lamp in hand, made his last rounds of the day. The nine prisoners in Madison's jail were resting quietly or were sound asleep. Satisfied that all was well, the sheriff returned to his own quarters and went to bed. Suddenly the silence was shattered by wild shrieking. Wie, in his nightshirt, leaped out of bed, grabbed his lantern, and raced to the cells. Two young prisoners by the names of Foster and

Sheevy were gyrating wildly in their bunks, their eyes saucer-wide with fright.

Wie opened the cell door, went in, and demanded an explanation. The inmates said that just after they had blown out their light and settled down, they heard a noise in the hallway beyond their door. The noise increased to a deafening crescendo and then seemed to come through the iron door grating to surround them. Then, they said, a strong light filled the cell, and a ghost wailed and brushed against their bedclothes. They had not been able to make out any well-defined shape.

Wie listened intently to their story and, although he dismissed it as fanciful, he did concede that the young men were genuinely frightened. They begged the sheriff to move them out of that cell and into one occupied by a burly black man. Wie refused and left them to work out their own salvation.

The next night the same unearthly shrieks rent the stillness, but this time the jailer, snug in bed, did not bother to investigate. The inmates did get a chance, however, to tell their tale to a reporter. They claimed that the light had again filled their cell and that to escape both it and the wild wailing they dived into their bunks and wrapped their heads with the blankets.

Later, Wie told the newsman that, whatever the commotion was, he thought Foster had a hand in it. Young Foster had been accused of setting fire to the city's flour mills, and the sheriff was convinced that Foster spent all his time behind bars planning pranks to frighten the wits out of Sheevy. Yet, in this instance, both men seemed deeply upset by an experience for which there seemed to be no logical explanation.

Had the prisoners fabricated the story to gain attention and stir up excitement? Had the specters of dark deeds returned to haunt them? Or was the wailing ghost the vestige of a long-forgotten prisoner sentenced to roam forever the cold, gray halls of Madison's jail?

MADISON'S PHANTOM AXMAN

About a hundred years ago, farmer Albert J. Lamson lived near Lake Wingra in Madison. On a dark and starless spring night, he stepped out to his front porch and heard the unmistakable sounds of an ax—the clear, ringing, rhythmic sounds of an expert woodsman at work. As Lamson listened, he was certain that the sounds came from Bartlett Woods, now known as Noe Woods, on the southwest side of the University of Wisconsin Arboretum.

Lamson was puzzled. Why would anyone be felling a tree in the middle of the night? Yet he knew he was not mistaken. He heard the blade bite into the trunk of a forest goliath, stop occasionally, then resume.

The next day, curious to learn what was going on, Lamson climbed the fence near the present Curtis Prairie and the Arboretum Administration Area. Entering the woods, he searched the area thoroughly but found no ax marks on the trees, no wood chips anywhere on the ground.

Several nights later, hearing the woodchopper again at work, Lamson summoned his hired man, who also claimed to hear the unmistakable strokes of the ax. At dawn, the two men went into the woods, but found nothing.

Lamson questioned his friends and neighbors.

Several persons who had been driving their teams over the lonely road said they had also heard the noises. Some, like Lamson, also searched the woods but found no evidence of recent woodcutting.

Periodically, during that summer and fall, the sounds came from Bartlett Woods. And travelers, hearing the story, avoided the "ghost road" at night. A search party, with lanterns, was finally organized to go into the woods at night to locate the woodchopper, but after several faint-hearted volunteers dropped out, the hunt was canceled. Lamson, although not superstitious, did not choose to enter the dense woods alone after dark.

Then suddenly the woodchopper abandoned his night work. His identity and the purpose of his work were never learned and to this day remain a mystery.

MADISON'S OLD GHOST ROAD

To present-day Madison residents, Seminole Highway is a quiet residential street of spacious lawns and stately trees where the only ghost ever seen is a small child in a Halloween costume. But in the late 1800s, when the highway was known as Bryant Road, unearthly apparitions appeared to teamsters and foot travelers.

They described the ghost as a luminous white vapor that would appear suddenly from the brush on either side of the road, follow them for a short distance, and then vanish. Others claimed that the vapor took the form of an Indian on a pony that appeared from nowhere, walked behind them a little way, then disappeared.

Sometimes late at night people fancied that they

heard the clatter of a pony's hoof beats as the beast and its ghostly rider charged up and down the road in pursuit of someone or something remembered from a distant past.

The phantom never harmed anyone, nor was its identity ever learned. Some said it was the spirit of an Indian who had been killed by a white man or Indian foe and was seeking revenge. Others thought it was the spirit of a white man who had been buried in the cemetery near the Bryant barn at the east end of the highway. But no one knew the reason for his return. By the time the horse and wagon gave way to the automobile, the troublesome ghost had disappeared, leaving Madison's "ghost road" alive only in the archives of history.

THE STRANGE CASE OF HENRY JAMES BROPHY

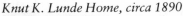

Knut K. Lunde Home, circa 1890

In 1909 Henry James Brophy was eleven years old. He lived with his grandparents, Mr. and Mrs. Knut K. Lunde of Mt. Horeb, and attended the village grade school. Like many shy, delicate children, he had few close friends. He also had no extraordinary talents . . . or so everyone thought. But a "talent" soon surfaced, the nature of which has never been satisfactorily explained. Either the boy was psychically gifted or he was a superb manipulator and clever fraud.

At noon on Tuesday, March 9, 1909, Henry arrived home from school for lunch. In opening the side door of his grandparents' home, he was struck in the back by a snowball that broke and splattered across the floor. The boy spun around, but there was no one in sight.

The next day, at the same time, the same thing happened. The Lundes checked the yard and sidewalk but found no assailant.

On Thursday evening of that week, cups suddenly flew from the dinner table and crashed to the floor, lamp chimneys disintegrated with no one touching them, spools of thread unwound, and bars of soap soared through the air. The family was terrorized, especially frail Mr. Lunde.

The following day, Henry's mother, Mrs. Patrick L. Trainor, arrived from Madison to attend a family funeral and spend the night with her parents and her sister, who also lived in the Lunde home. Early in the evening, Mrs. Trainor sat down to play the organ. In that instant, household utensils took to the air, banging against the walls and crashing to the floor. Lunde became so agitated that the family sent for the Reverend Mostrom. The minister came promptly, bringing Sam Thompson with him. As the two men entered the house, a hymnal that had been lying on a windowsill near the door fell to the floor at their feet. The Lundes screamed, "There, you see it!"

The Reverend Mostrom listened attentively to the story and tried to find a rational explanation for the manifestations. When someone mentioned that the playing of the organ had seemed to activate the objects, the minister sat down to play. Thompson walked the floor with the boy at his side. Suddenly Henry yelled, "Look out!" A large butcher knife left the table, arced through the air, and fell at their feet. Thompson said later that the boy could not have touched it. The same phenomenon occurred with a hat pin. Although the two visitors remained skeptical, they were unable to explain what they had seen. Neither man slept that night.

Nightly thereafter, objects flew around the rooms. Doors crashed to the floor after the screws holding their hinges were removed by unseen forces, lids flew off the wood stove, and chimneys of the kerosene lamps broke as soon as they were set into place. A drawer in a sewing machine came free and soared high in the room, scattering bobbins, spools of thread, and needles in every direction and knocking plaster from a wall. A table knife, flying through the air, struck the floor at the grandmother's feet, and an ornament from a heating stove was pulled loose and thrown across the room. When family members retired for the night, showers of coal fell upon them.

News of the phenomena spread rapidly beyond the confines of the little Norwegian town, attracting the attention of clairvoyants, curiosity-seekers, and newsmen. On a single night two hundred people streamed through the Lunde house, leaving tracks of muddy footprints. They saw no manifestations, only damage said to have been done by flying household objects.

If the Lundes could not explain what was happening in their home, some of Mt. Horeb's residents believed they could. Two prominent citizens said that because the large brick house had both electricity and telephone it had become "electrified." They claimed that this electrification was causing the disturbances and insisted upon cutting the electric wires to put an end to the "spell." But the distraught family, fearing darkness more than the chaos, tossed the intruders out.

Finally, because the phenomena always occurred in Henry's presence and because the flying objects always seemed to travel toward the child, the family concluded that he must somehow be responsible for them. They reasoned that if Henry were removed from the house and the strange manifestations continued, then perhaps electricity was the cause.

The boy was accordingly sent to Springdale to visit his uncles, Hans and Andrew Lunde. Henry spent one day at Hans's house during which time only a few small objects took flight. At Andrew's home, the poltergeist activity increased. No sooner had Henry entered the house than a pail of water began spinning, then spilled across the kitchen floor. After that had been mopped up, Henry, spying a mirror on the wall, said, "You better take that down." The older man laughed. A moment later, the mirror crashed to the floor.

Meanwhile, all was peaceful at the Mt. Horeb home. Mrs. Lunde, however, anxious to find some rational explanation for the phenomena, had been discussing the matter with a Mt. Horeb cheesemaker during her grandson's absence. The merchant told her that in the old country a bag of salt was the time-honored remedy to exorcise evil spirits. Word was sent to Springdale and a bag of salt was placed in Henry's pocket. The day after this was done a neighbor boy came over to play. The salt left Henry's pocket and struck the visitor in the face. Taken back only momentarily, the visitor stayed and the two boys played marbles, but not for long. The marbles disappeared before their eyes and only Henry knew where they had gone. By some means, he always found them, even those tucked deep into quilts on the beds. After the neighbor boy left, Andrew tried an experiment. He held a cigar box of marbles before his nephew, who sat facing him on a chair. The marbles leaped from the box; the startled uncle said the boy had never touched them.

That night when Henry was in bed, a noise erupted from the wall next to his bed. Andrew examined the wall but found nothing to account for the disturbance. When the noise continued, he checked outside; there was nothing. He came back inside and Henry said, "You better look out or the plaster will fall on you." Andrew moved the boy to a couch across the room. A neighbor woman who was visiting sat down on one edge of the couch and got up promptly. The couch had begun vibrating.

In the morning, Andrew found a large hole in the plastered wall next to the bed where Henry had lain. He was perplexed, yet fearful of having the boy remain in the house any longer. Hans agreed to take Henry back to Mt. Horeb and, upon their arrival at the Lunde home, the uncle witnessed an unusual manifestation. Hans said, "I took a basket of eggs along and set them on a chair in the house. While we were standing there one egg flew out of the basket and struck Henry in the face. I saw it leave the basket with my own eyes and there was no one anywhere near the basket. Two more eggs jumped out of the basket on the floor and one jumped off the table."

The family, in desperation, consulted a number of physicians. It had been noted that the child was running a high fever and was losing weight. According to his mother, he was also experiencing moody, cross spells during which times he refused to have anything to do with anyone. The doctors thought the manifestations were delusions or fakes. Churchmen were less certain. A prayer meeting was held one evening at the Lunde house to exorcise the unseen forces, but it resulted only in an increase in manifestations.

Finally, it was decided to have Henry examined by Dr. George Kingsley of Madison, who was a spiritualist and a physician. Otto Dahle, who was on his way to Milwaukee on business, accompanied Henry to Kingsley's office. During the few minutes that the boy was in the office, the doctor pronounced him a splendid medium for his age, destined to become one of the world's greatest spiritualists. He explained that Henry did not yet have the spirits under control, but that he would gain control of them later.

Other clairvoyants were more specific. They saw three spirits—two women and one man—hovering near the child. They did not explain who the spirits were. Henry's mother recalled that when her son was small he had been cared for by two women spiritualists, one of whom later died. Could she have passed on to the child her supernatural powers? Some people thought so. The seers also said that the three spirits were oppressed by crowds; for that reason, the manifestations never occurred when Henry was in school or when large groups of people came to the house. But the Lundes had come to a different conclusion. They told Mert P. Peavy, local editor of the *Dodgeville Chronicle*, that they believed Henry had been hypnotized by someone and left in hypnotic trance.

If many accepted the notion that Henry James Brophy was a wonder boy, possessed of strange powers resulting from either a hypnotic state or spiritualistic gift, others did not. Among the detractors were Dr. N.C. Evans and former Sheriff G.E. Mickelson. These two visited the Lundes one night at the peak of the excitement. They were seated with their backs to the kitchen doorway when two pieces of sausage, a piece of soap, and chunks of coal flew into the room from the kitchen. They knew that Henry was in the kitchen, and when they asked why he did not come out, the grandparents said he was shy of visitors. Evans then whirled around and asked Henry, who stood in the doorway, if he had thrown the articles. He said Henry did not deny doing so.

On another evening, Evans was in the sitting room with the Lunde women, and Henry was again in the kitchen. Suddenly a ball of yarn sailed into the room. The doctor was convinced that it had been thrown by someone in the kitchen.

When Dr. Clarke Gapen was asked for his opinion, he said, "It is nonsense to waste any time on such cases unless it be to explode or expose them. They can always be explained away and have been time and again exposed."

Yet parapsychologists do not believe that all cases can be easily explained away, nor do they believe it is nonsense to spend time developing theories that might lead to an understanding of poltergeist activity. Experts agree that young children are often the focus of a "noisy ghost," and at least one researcher believes that a child unconsciously creates such disturbances to vent repressed hostility. Henry had lived with his grandparents since he was two years old. Did the loss of daily contact with his mother and the mother's remarriage have a negative effect upon him that was unconsciously expressed in propelling objects through the air? It's known too that poltergeist activity is prevalent among youngsters having histories of physical illness. As a baby, Henry had been run over by a wagon and crippled. Although he finally recovered from the accident, he remained delicate and sickly. Was the psyche overcompensating for physical weakness?

Today only a handful of Mt. Horeb residents who remember Henry are still alive, and their remembrances are dimmed by time. Josie Evans thinks the poltergeist business was all a fake. Her brother, Jake, thinks maybe it was not. They both agree they don't know for certain what did happen. Mabel Espeseth says a lot of the stories were made up. She lived for a while in the Lunde house and claims that she never gave a thought to supernatural activity. But Jan Kogen, who had also lived in the house, recalls that strange things happened every day for a year. A camera the family owned kept taking pictures on its own and finally had to be replaced. Edwin Offerdahl of rural Mt. Horeb says that Henry got rid of "it," whatever it was. He and Henry had worked for the railroad after school and Offerdahl believes that Henry got married and moved to California. Others recall that he had gone to Madison or Milwaukee. No one in the community knows whether Henry is still living or whether he ever came back to Mt. Horeb since he left in 1914 or 1915.

Only one thing is certain: Henry James Brophy created a sensation in this little Norwegian village west of Madison. Wittingly or unwittingly, he built a memorial to himself that no one who knew him has ever forgotten. And how he did it will never be known.

THE LEGEND OF GHOST HILL

Only a few people alive today in Dane County's Burke Township recall the origin of the mysterious specter that haunted Ghost Hill. That protrusion of earth was on the former Messerschmidt farm in the northeast corner of section 19 on the old road from Madison to Token Creek.

What gave rise to the hill's ghostly legend? Early residents claimed that at the stroke of midnight each evening, a human figure clad completely in white would appear astride a white horse. It would race across the top of the hill, or sometimes across its base, going in the direction of Blooming Grove. Regardless of the weather or darkness of night, the horseman could be seen plainly, its white cape stretched out in the breeze like some spectral streamer.

Who—or what—was this phantom? There is no definite explanation of its origin. Some witnesses thought it was the angry spirit of an early pioneer who had been robbed and murdered near the hill. The man's ghost was condemned to wander through the night, seeking revenge for the brutal death.

At least one documented effort was made to identify the ghost—or at least verify its existence. A Madison resident named George Armbrecht told a

Wisconsin State Journal reporter in September 1936 that he and several other brave companions camped on the hill one night to see the horseman. Midnight came but unfortunately no ghost appeared.

The hill was partially demolished when a quarry was opened to supply stone for the Madison airport, and the legend of the horseman of Ghost Hill has nearly vanished from Burke Township.

Part IV.
Ghosts of the Kettle Moraine

The Phantom Rider of Pumpkin Hollow

As dusk settles on quiet autumn nights over the south line road in the village of Oak Hill, near Sullivan, old-timers say a ghostly Indian brave still gallops through the gathering darkness. His pony is fast, and wears a garland of sliced pumpkin around its neck. A whole pumpkin encircles the barrel of the Indian's musket, which he carries high above his head. The legend of the phantom rider begins in early pioneer days and bears more than a casual resemblance to Washington Irving's "Legend of Sleepy Hollow."

Harry Osgood operated a tavern on the south line road frequented by ox drivers and travelers on their way to Milwaukee. The structure was little more than a log shelter along the rutted trail. Nevertheless, it was a favorite stop.

Early one fall evening, an Indian arrived at the tavern astride a lively pinto pony. The man was tipsy but somehow managed his way into the establishment and demanded more whiskey. Osgood refused the request, fearing the consequences of such an act. Instead, he gave the brave a number of ripe, bright orange pumpkins. The Indian was delighted and proceeded to impale the largest pumpkin on the barrel of his rifle. He cut the others into chunks and with some string draped them around his pony's neck. Pleased with his work, he set off down the road.

A short way off, Doc Powers, a pioneer physician in the region, was riding toward the tavern after making calls at several homesteads. As he gazed down the trail, he saw the pumpkin-bedecked Indian galloping toward him. The trail was narrow near the spot where the two met. Powers demanded to pass first but the Indian refused. Instead, he bashed the physician over the head with the rifle and Powers fell from his horse.

What happened next is unclear. Some say the physician recovered his senses and grabbed the rifle from the Indian, smashing the weapon on a tree trunk until it was bent. With the remnants, Powers pummeled the youth until the Indian fled across the marsh. Both horses bolted into the forest. Powers knew that men from the tavern would help in finding his horse.

Another version of the story claims the doctor lay unconscious for some time. When he awoke, pieces of pumpkin littered the road, but the Indian was nowhere to be seen. The doctor's horse was found a short way off.

Whichever version is correct, Doc Powers swore vengeance on the Indian who attacked him. Powers made his way to the tavern, where proprietor Osgood agreed to help him in the search for the horse. When the pair reached the spot where the attack had occurred, Powers shook his head over the chunks of pumpkin scattered about. He said the name of the area really ought to be changed from Pleasant Valley to Pumpkin Hollow. And so it was.

The Indian was never seen again at the tavern or anywhere in the region. Wayfarers, however, frequently reported the ghost of an Indian bedecked with pumpkins galloping up and down the south line road for many years. And, some say, when the chill autumn wind scatters brittle leaves down Pumpkin Hollow, the Indian brave can still be seen in his garish costume.

The Death of August

In the nineteenth century, before the era of instant communication, the Gottlieb family farmed near Fremont. One evening after the children had gone to bed, Gottlieb and his wife heard thumping sounds upstairs, sounds that seemed to travel from room to room. Before the parents could investigate, the children, awake and frightened, tumbled downstairs. Then the sounds ceased. Gottlieb, however, was determined to find the cause. Taking a lamp in one hand and a stick in the other, he climbed the staircase. He searched all the rooms but found nothing that could have accounted for the mysterious noises. Unless...

Back downstairs, Gottlieb turned to his wife and said quietly, "My brother is dead."

Twenty-four hours later, a messenger brought the news of August Gottlieb's death. He had died in his home thirty miles away. His relatives had not known that he had been ill and dying.

At the funeral, Gottlieb learned that brother August had died at the precise time that the thumpings were heard.

The Possession of Carl Seige

Can an evil spirit take over a person's mind, body, and soul? Man has always thought so. In every culture, in every period of history, demonic possession has been recognized. Loud, obscene curses issue from the mouth of the victim, his body contorts, and his eyes gleam with hatred. Often, his environment is beset by paranormal manifestations—

poundings in the walls, levitation of furniture, and the presence of fireballs.

The causes of demonic possession are little understood, but the condition seems to occur in individuals with weak egos, unmet psychological needs, or some obscure, if undetected, character flaw. Since possession closely resembles some forms of mental illness, medical treatment is usually tried first. For intractable cases that do not respond to medication, the religious rite of exorcism may be performed to cast out the "demons." No one knows how many exorcisms are performed in this country in a given year (one source says 125 during 1975) because the possessed usually insist upon anonymity. But Carl Seige, of Watertown, was not so fortunate. He was harassed by demons for twenty years and the whole town knew it. His exorcism, along with more lurid details of his sensational case, was reported by Milwaukee newspapers and reprinted by papers in other parts of the state.

The diabolical manifestations first appeared in 1848. Carl was then five years old and living with his family in their native Germany. One day one of Carl's sisters found a duck's egg under a tree beside the door of their small hut. With typical childlike curiosity, the girl picked up the egg and took it to her mother. Mrs. Seige noticed that the egg had a small pinhole in one end. She cautioned her daughter to put the egg back where she had found it. The girl did. At that moment, the family dog appeared, seized the egg, and ate it. Immediately, he was stricken blind and, raging with fright, ran in wide circles through the yard. The child fled, screaming. The dog was promptly shot.

A short time later, the little girl was seized with blindness and spasms and soon was bedridden. She lingered in agony for a year. After her death, Carl was attacked with blindness and severe pains that continued for a number of months, leaving him lame and with a withered hand twisted into a grotesque shape. But he would manage. His sight was partially restored. And his life had been spared.

But when Carl turned twelve, uncontrollable seizures set in. His head was jerked like a puppet by unseen forces, his shoulders twitched, and he was often thrown violently to the ground where he struck out at all who tried to approach him. He frothed at the mouth and his eyes filled with malevolence. If a "fit" overtook him while eating, his hands struck his dinner plate, upsetting it and scattering food all over the floor. Sometimes a spell would last an entire day. Between attacks, he prayed for deliverance and made the sign of the cross. But his prayers went unanswered. So did those of his pious Lutheran family. The German doctors, using roots and herbs and all the medicines available at that time, were unable to cure, or even alleviate, the dreadful symptoms of Carl's strange malady.

Finally, in the spring of 1867, when Carl was twenty-four, the despairing family—father, mother, three sons, and five daughters—immigrated to the German community of Watertown, Wisconsin. But troubles followed them. The sixteen-year-old daughter, a beautiful young woman, was sent to live in the home of the local Lutheran minister to help with the housework and the care of the family's several children. Before long, she became pregnant by the minister and bore a son. In sorrow and shame, she returned to her own family.

But her return precipitated a series of terrifying events. Her brother's demonic symptoms greatly increased. Now the violence was focused upon the baby. Screaming that he intended to kill the infant, Carl would spring toward the child with eyes wild in his pale face and froth glistening on his lips. His sister, terror-stricken, clutched the baby and ran from the room. She slept only fitfully at night, keeping the infant close, and during the day she never let it out of her sight. As fears and tensions built, the entire family suffered strange, recurring illnesses marked by dizziness and severe headaches.

In the evenings, unearthly noises shook the house. Open doors would slam shut with no one near them, the window panes rattled loudly, even on windless nights, and weird, hollow noises emanated from one of the rooms. Seige inspected the house thoroughly and found nothing that could account for the phenomena. Late one evening, to the family's horror, an enormous ball of fire appeared on the top of the cooking stove. As they watched, frozen with fear, Carl dashed forward and struck the fireball with his fist. It broke apart, scattering small glowing spheres into all corners of the room. Yet, nothing was burned, and the fires gradually disappeared.

Shortly after this incident, the family cow, tied in the back yard, started behaving strangely. She began to rear on her hind legs, smite her tail, and shake her horns with savage fury. Carl, watching her from the kitchen window, gave great shouts of joy. Seige could not get near the beast to milk her, and he and his wife were convinced that somehow the demons had gotten into the cow.

The peasant family, who had sought sanctuary in the New World from the evil, supernatural forces that beleaguered them, were engulfed by fear and despair. At first they had tried to keep Carl's illness a secret. But as his attacks increased with awesome intensity, Seige knew that he must seek outside help. In the winter of 1868, he called in a Dr. Quinney, son of a prominent Stockbridge Indian chief.

Quinney listened to the young man's history, then administered an herb physic. He also applied poultices to Carl's shoulders in an attempt to draw out the evil spirits. When the compresses were removed the next day, they were covered with bristles! These bristles were of different colors and ranged in size from half an inch to three inches in length. The Indian doctor could not account for them. But an explanation was offered later by the spirit of a long-deceased Mohawk Indian speaking through a Milwaukee medium. This spirit claimed that the bristles were actually "long, hairy worms generated by microscopic animals" found in a spring in Germany, whose waters Carl had drunk as a child. The spirit said that these worms were feeding upon Carl's muscles and would eventually kill him.

The parents were not so sure. Some time after the bristles appeared, Carl had a violent seizure during which he gave the names of the devils possessing him. One was named Wilhelm Buhrer. Seige recalled that Buhrer was a desperate man who had murdered a hog drover in Germany many years ago for his money. Was the soul of the murderer embodied in a hog? And was this evil entity tormenting Carl? Perhaps this accounted for the presence of the bristles. Some people thought so.

When Dr. Quinney could offer no further help, the family turned to a spiritualist medium. He arrived at the house to find Carl black in the face and gasping for breath. It seems that a snake was inside the young man, pushing its head up into his throat. The lashings of its tail were believed to be felt under Carl's ribs! The medium pushed a goose quill down Carl's throat, then waved the quill over his head. Finally, Carl became quiet and was helped into bed. Relief, however, was short-lived.

When the demons returned, the Seiges decided to appeal to the local priest. He declined to intervene, however, because Carl was not a Catholic. When the Catholic bishop visited Watertown and heard the story, however, he agreed to arrange for an exorcism.

In early November 1869, Carl was brought to the Catholic church in Watertown for the rites. The church was filled. Catholics, Protestants, and those of no particular religious persuasion crammed the pews. An awesome hush spread over the congregation as Carl Seige was laid upon the altar. His face was wan and drawn, his slender, wasted body almost corpselike in appearance. Seven priests, in cassocks, white surplices, and purple stoles, took their places beside the stricken man. Their faces held no fear, yet each, in his heart, recognized the dangers inherent in the ritual—of engaging in conversation with the demons, of being attacked psychologically in such ways that they themselves might be possessed by the evil spirits they sought to cast out.

"Almighty Father, Everlasting God . . ."

They recited in unison, each priest tracing the sign of the cross over the young man's head.

"We beseech thee, this day, to help us cast out from thy beloved servant, Carl Seige . . ."

Each priest sprinkled holy water upon the victim.

" . . . those demons that torment and seek to destroy . . . and by thy infinite mercy . . ."

Each priest laid hands upon the prostrate form before them.

"In the name of the Father, and of the Son, and of the Holy Ghost . . ."

Then came the Latin words of ancient prayers, powerful incantations used for centuries to drive evil from the earth. The holy men knelt in a circle around Carl. At the back of the altar a picture of the Holy Virgin glowed in the candlelight, and flanking her were orbs of burning incense giving off a heavy, pungent fragrance.

The prayers, the sprinklings of holy water, the sign of the cross were repeated—over and over with soft, yet urgent insistence.

Suddenly Carl's head jerked, and from his gaping mouth the evil spirit spewed invectives. It shouted obscenities in German, threatening to surround the church with its own water, which it would purify. The forces of God and Satan had met. The priests' faces, shadowed by the flickering candlelight, were set like stone in mortar. The demon laughed raucously at the prayers, telling the priests they had not yet found the right one. Then it began speaking in tongues—snatches of Irish and Latin mingled with strange utterings that resembled no spoken language. Undeterred, the priests continued their prayers, beads of sweat sparkling their brows. They spoke with confidence, with a discipline born of long training. And the congregation watched, moved, unmoving.

When the last cold rays of the setting sun vanished below the windowsills of the church, the exorcism was halted. The exhausted priests were cautiously optimistic—four demons had been cast out. But there were more.

On the next day, Carl was again placed upon the altar before the picture of the Holy Virgin, and the priests began once more the long ritual. Three more demons were cast out.

And on the third, and final, day, the last demon agreed to leave if all the persons assembled would leave with him. All but three acquiesced and, to the great joy and relief of Carl, the churchmen, and the congregation, the devil departed. The miracle had been made manifest.

A subdued and grateful Carl, along with his family, joined the Catholic church. They hung a crucifix on the wall and bought prayer books and rosaries. And Carl attended mass each morning.

One month later, however, another devil appeared. This one was successfully cast out, but not before shouting, with glee, that four more demons remained.

Here, the story of the possessed man fades from the newspapers. In 1870, the press had more important stories to write. Wisconsin communities were astir with the issuance of railway bonds, and overseas Napoleon III was marching his troops across the face of Europe to touch off the Franco-Prussian War. No matter. The sensationalism created by the possession of Carl Seige had already peaked.

No one now living witnessed Carl's exorcism. Nor can anyone ever know the nature or the dimensions of his illness. Was he mentally ill? Or was he really possessed by supernatural, earthbound entities who invaded his mind, body, and soul to torment him with their evil thoughts and fears? Today's physicians would probably have diagnosed Carl as an epileptic.

There is one postscript to the story of the Seige family. The minister who had fathered Carl's nephew was arrested on a charge of seduction and committed to the county jail. After being confined for a month, he tore his blankets into strips and hanged himself in his cell. It is said that the boy and his mother lived on happily in her parents' home.

THE VOICE ON THE BRIDGE

In the 1870s, the village of Omro, west of Oshkosh, was the center of Spiritualist activity in the state. Here the First Spiritualist's Society hosted eminent spiritualists and mediums from all over the United States—the Davenport brothers, Moses Hull of Boston, Benjamin Todd of Michigan, Susan Johnson of California, and many others. Seances multiplied and spirits materialized, but, with peculiar irony, the combined efforts of local and visiting mediums failed to solve the murder of a local citizen.

It was about 1877 that John Sullivan, a local farmer, was mysteriously slain. Sometime between nine and ten o'clock at night, he left the village where he had spent the day trading. It had been a long, weary day, and his thoughts were on home and bed as he trudged over the bridge spanning the Fox River.

Suddenly a cry of alarm rang out, followed by the discharge of a gun. A short time later Sullivan was found dead at the side of the bridge. There were no witnesses, no known motives, no suspects. Law enforcement officials were baffled. Who killed John Sullivan? Seances buzzed with the question as candles flickered late into the night in the homes of the psychics. But there was never an answer.

Then one night a Mr. Wilson was crossing the

bridge where the farmer had met his death. Out of the darkness, he noticed a man just ahead of him shouldering a gun. A voice whispered into Wilson's ear, "That is the gun that killed John Sullivan." A terror-filled scream, then a loud report rent the air. And the apparition vanished.

Wilson fled to the village to relate his experience, swearing that he would recognize the murder weapon if he ever saw it again. Later he claimed that he had seen it. Who owned it? Wilson would not say. The spirits weren't talking either, and to this day Sullivan's murder remains a mystery.

Mrs. Courtney's Return

Mr. and Mrs. William Courtney lived in an area of Vinland known as Brooks' Corners, about seven miles north of Oshkosh. The couple had never gotten along well, and it was reported that Mrs. Courtney had left her Canadian-Irish husband at least once. But she eventually returned to live with him in a state of uneasy truce.

On November 4, 1873, Mrs. Courtney died. She was alone in the bedroom, her husband busy in another part of the house. Upon discovering the corpse, Courtney immediately moved out of the house and into the home of his mother-in-law, who lived about a mile away. He returned only periodically to do the chores.

He did retain the hired girl, but not for long. Several days after the funeral, the servant heard sharp rappings on the windowpanes in a room adjoining the room in which her employer's wife had died. The girl jumped back from the windows. Silence. Then the rat-tat-tat again on the panes. She lifted a corner of the curtain and peered out. No one was there. Badly frightened, she fled to a neighbor's house and vowed never to return.

Shortly thereafter, Hiram Mericle and his family, who lived about five hundred feet from Courtney's house, noticed a light burning within. Knowing the place to be vacant, Mericle and some members of his family went to the house and discovered that the light was burning in the room in which Mrs. Courtney had died. As they drew closer, the light dimmed and finally went out. Puzzled, they returned home. Then about three o'clock in the morning they spotted the light again, shining brightly as before.

Some time later, other neighbors noticed lights in the Courtney house and went to investigate. Suddenly a very bright light appeared, and a shadowy form passed in front of it. Someone screamed, "Look, it's Mrs. Courtney!"

From that moment on, the residents of Brooks' Corners knew that the house was occupied by a being not of this world. Lights of varying shapes and forms continued to appear regularly. Sometimes they were circles about six or seven inches in diameter, with smaller lights circling the large ones. At other times they took oval shapes. The most startling observation was that the light did not reflect, but was simply a flame with clearly defined edges, while all around was inky darkness.

The lights were seen in all parts of the main building and also in the one-story rear addition to the house that was the kitchen. Sometimes they were unusually brilliant; at other times they were dim.

On November 20, the *Oshkosh Weekly Times* heard of the phenomena. The paper promptly dispatched a reporter and companion by horse and buggy to check out the story.

By nightfall, the men had reached the house of Jacob Whitacre, who lived half a mile from Courtney's. They ate supper with the Whitacres and listened to the stories told by the family, every one of whom had seen the lights. The reporter found the family to be intelligent, straightforward people who had obviously seen something for which there seemed to be no normal explanation.

After supper, Whitacre led his guests to the mystery house. A group of about a hundred boys and men had already gathered there in the deep snow, stamping their feet to keep warm and comparing notes on what each had seen. The reporter saw a bright light appear suddenly in one of the windows. Just as quickly it vanished, plunging the house into darkness. Gusts of wind churned the snowdrifts, and finally the men, becoming cold and disappointed at not seeing further manifestations, turned back to Mericle's house to warm up. They made a second trip back to Courtney's and arrived in time to see a series of bright lights exploding like flashes of lightning, to be followed again by total darkness.

On November 21 and 22, large crowds converged upon the haunted house, but no lights appeared. The Oshkosh newsman speculated that since a family had planned to move into the house no more lights of a ghostly nature would be seen.

In December, the reporter interviewed Courtney, who claimed that the lights were of human intervention. He said that he had left the cellar door open so that anyone could have gained access to the house; he also said that one day he had found the kitchen door kicked in. And the motive for the lights? Courtney thought probably someone wanted to rent the place and was trying to scare off the man to whom he had already promised it.

Were pranksters at work? The hundreds of witnesses to the "light shows" did not think so. Who would brave the wild winds and deep snows to enter a vacant house in such a remote area . . . night after night? Observers saw light that did not reflect. Light that flashed like lightning. Light that changed shape and that was sometimes surrounded by a halo of smaller lights. Could the kerosene lantern of that era perform in such bizarre ways? It seems unlikely.

Then did the visitors who crowded the homes of Hiram Mericle and Jacob Whitacre every night from six o'clock until midnight all fantasize in order to create a little excitement during a cold, bleak winter?

Or were the lights of supernatural origin, signaling the return of Mrs. Courtney? Did she come back, in spectral form, to enjoy a few hours of peace and solitude in the place that, in life, had brought her so much unhappiness?

MURDER ON THE BOARDWALK

Back in the 1890s, Oshkosh was a bustling frontier city that spilled across the plain. Sawmills on both banks of the Fox River hummed incessantly, turning out pine lumber and shingles while factories produced finished wood products. Lumberjacks roared into town on pay day and their heavy drinking in Main Street saloons often ended in brawls.

One night a rural man who had been shopping in the city started homeward carrying a rocking chair. His young son accompanied him. The sidewalks at that time were high boardwalks, and as the pair passed a large grove of gnarled oak trees, the father decided to rest for a moment. He put down the chair and, elated over the splendid bargain he had struck with the shopkeeper, sat down to rock.

Suddenly, from out of the darkness beyond the trees, two drunks appeared. Resentful of the man's obvious delight in his new chair, and spoiling for a fight, they taunted the stranger. The quarrel soon got out of hand and the drunks killed the man and ran off.

The boy, meanwhile, had dived under the boardwalk. When the assailants left, the child raced across the street for help. By the time the neighbors arrived, the father was dead in his chair.

For years afterward, travelers claimed that they heard the creaks of the rocker and the groans of the dying man in the grove where he had been slain. And those who are keen of ear say that the eerie sounds can still be heard, carried by the wild wind of a stormy night.

The Night Stalker

The winter nights were long and lonely for the families of lumberjacks. They remained behind while the men labored in the great northern forests during the last century. The women and children lived in scores of small settlements scattered across the state, hardly more than clusters of log dwellings separated by miles of wilderness and snow-choked trails. The villages were as isolated as any spot on earth for months at a time.

One such village was West Algoma, a pioneer village near Lake Winnebago and since incorporated into the city of Oshkosh. But nearly a century ago, the isolation and barren tranquility of that isolated outpost was broken by the terrifying appearance of a mysterious man dressed all in black. The figure came each night to West Algoma that winter, swathed in black cape and clothing from head to toe. He was of enormous height and walked slowly with the aid of a crooked wooden cane.

The stranger's routine never varied. At the stroke of midnight he would emerge from the darkness at the edge of town, stride slowly down the wooden sidewalk, and vanish into the night. He never spoke or altered his gait. The walk lasted precisely ninety minutes, the route never changed, and his arrival and departure times changed by only a few seconds. Townsfolk hid behind barred doors and curtained windows, afraid to interfere with or question the stalker. Few slept until the nocturnal visitor had gone. On one particular night, however, a young boy reportedly approached the stranger. The youth stole a glance at the figure in the bright moonlight. Beneath the dark hat was a pallid, expressionless face seemingly devoid of life. The boy fled in terror.

Night after night, week after week of that long winter, the stranger would walk the streets of West Algoma. But the day in spring when the menfolk returned from the piney woods he vanished, never to return. Who was he? To this day, no one knows. He did no harm. Was he sent to protect the women and children? A ghostly town crier keeping watch over the sleeping families until the men returned?

Then again, the night stalker may have been

the product of some villager's fanciful imagination in an effort to keep the children amused and close to home on those cold, desolate nights.

THE HAUNTED MUSEUM

Visitors to the Paine Art Center in Oshkosh marvel at the opulent splendor of Russian and Greek icons, Remington sculptures, and period furnishings that span three centuries. Yet many say that the great hall, the sitting room, the library, the dining room do not resemble a museum at all; they look more like the rooms of a house that is actually lived in, as if the family in residence had just stepped out for a moment. But no one lives here . . . or do they?

At one time, lumber baron Nathan Paine had clearly intended to live here with his wife, Jesse Kimberly, heiress to the paper fortunes. It was Nathan's dream to build an eighteenth century English Tudor manor house that would be the pride of "Sawdust City" and that would be donated, ultimately, to the city as an art center. New York architect Bryant Fleming designed the house, while interior decorator Phelps D. Jewett planned the furnishings with meticulous taste. Construction began in 1927 and even the stock market crash two years later did not deter work on the $800,000 mansion. By 1932, however, Nathan was depleted of funds, and he closed the doors of the Paine Lumber Company, the largest sash and door company in the world. When he recovered financially, he restarted work on the house instead of reopening the factory. This move generated bitter criticism by his unemployed workers, most of whom had always regarded him as a ruthless and exploitive entrepreneur.

When the house was nearly completed, Nathan and his wife received a bomb threat—if they moved in, the place would be blown up. A threat made, perhaps, by an angry employee? No bomb was ever planted. But the Paines never lived in the house at 1410 Algoma Boulevard. In 1947, Nathan died. And in 1948, the Paine Art Center, funded by Nathan's estate, was opened to the public.

And the resident? An unknown poltergeist who was thought to have "moved in" sometime during the 1930s. Employees have found furniture in the attic rearranged from time to time. One staff member, standing at the top of the attic stairs, claims to have witnessed the flutter of pages of Nathan Paine's open journals. And at least two others say they have heard low moanings when alone in the building.

Does the ghost of Nathan's Yankee grandfather, Edward Paine, haunt his grandson's home? It

The Paine Art Center

was Edward who brought the family west from New York in 1853 to set up the sawmill on the banks of the Fox River. Or is it the ghost of Nathan's father, George, watching over his son's property, keeping it safe for all time? No one knows for sure, but the tales linger as muted footnotes to the history of a bygone era.

FOOTSTEPS IN THE DARK

The house at the crest of High Street in Pewaukee projects the solidity of a medieval fort. Built in the nineteenth century when the octagon craze swept the Midwest, the three-story, eight-sided cement structure, with walls eighteen inches thick, has a permanence about it that contemporary houses lack. Yet the severity of its lines is softened by the dark wood framing, long windows, the carpenter's lace that embellishes a second-floor porch, and the towering ash and maple trees that surround it. To the casual observer, the house appears to be only an intriguing architectural folly; to those familiar with its history, it is remembered as the house of haunting footsteps—the abode of some unseen, unknown, ghostly night walker.

The site originally held a log house. But after this structure burned to the ground, Deacon West, a blacksmith, bought the property and had a house erected on it in the late 1850s. Several years later, West too lost his home in a devastating fire. Only the massive walls remained.

The next owner, Ira Rowe, sold the place to N. P. Iglehart, a colonel from Kentucky. Iglehart, who spent his summers in Pewaukee, rebuilt the house into its present form in about 1873. He also discovered springs on the property and soon established a small home business, bottling the water and selling it under the label Oakton Springs Water.

In the early 1900s, Audrey D. Hyle, a Milwaukee attorney, owned the house. And it was during his ownership that the unearthly footsteps were first heard. Someone or something wandered through the vast rooms and corridors each night at exactly 10:45. It was never seen and it never bothered anyone. Sleeping residents were sometimes half awakened, but drifted back into sleep as the footsteps faded.

In the 1930s, Mr. and Mrs. Joseph Zupet lived in the haunted house, and by this time the nocturnal visitor had varied its wanderings slightly. It now ascended the staircase from the front hall to the second floor at precisely

Octagon House

10:50 P.M. and descended by another staircase into the garden at precisely 1:20 A.M. Sometimes it paused outside a closed bedroom door, then moved on down the wide hallway. Whatever it was searching for was never known. Nothing was ever disturbed and nothing was ever taken.

Nevertheless, the Zupets became apprehensive about their resident ghost and invited a mystic by the name of Koran to visit their home. He was performing at a Milwaukee theater at the time and welcomed the opportunity to make the twenty-mile trip to Pewaukee. Koran made a thorough investigation and, although he did not identify the unseen guest, he did assure the homeowners that it was a friendly one. But after three years of residence, the Zupets put the house up for sale.

Tales of the haunted house spread, however, and no one wanted to live there. For a number of years the octagon house remained vacant. The housing shortage of World War II brought a succession of renters, and finally, in 1948, Mr. and Mrs. John T. Oswald of Milwaukee bought the house and lived in it until 1966, when they sold it to the present owners.

Insofar as is known, neither family was ever visited by the mysterious, if friendly, phantom.

THE HILLE CURSE

Mrs. Dorothy Ransome knows exactly who the phantom is that approaches her farmhouse near Waukesha, Wisconsin, and then vanishes at the kitchen door. The ghost's name is John Hille, and he built the house over a century ago. What the ghost of John Hille may not know is that his recent appearances are just the latest chapters in a saga of bizarre, and often tragic, events that have led many to believe the farm now called Ravensholme is cursed. Over a dozen people associated with the farm, including seven members of the John Hille family and two of Mrs. Ransome's grandchildren, have met with strange, untimely deaths.

Mrs. Ransome and her husband, Ralph, have lived on the farm since 1971, although they purchased the property in 1948. The ghost of John Hille has been making regular trips to their back door since the early 1970s. It was after the ghost's first appearance that Mrs. Ransome began delving into the history of the farm. She discovered a chilling legacy.

The history of the farmstead began in 1848, the year Wisconsin was admitted to the Union. John Hille, thirty-seven years old at the time, brought his young wife, Magdalena, and several children to settle the 146 acres of virgin wilderness bordering the Fox River, six miles southwest of Waukesha. Hille had been born in Hanover, Germany, and immigrated to America in 1837 following the deaths of both parents. He apprenticed to a cabinetmaker in his native city and brought that skill to New York where he worked until his move to the Wisconsin frontier. Magdalena Jaquiltard Hille was also an immigrant. She met and subsequently married John in 1837, five years after her own family reached the East Coast from France.

The Hilles began their new life near Waukesha in a log cabin. Gradually they built their holdings into a prosperous 215-acre farm with several granaries, barns, sheds, and a spacious stone farmhouse constructed with granite boulders Hille cleared from nearby fields.

By 1880 the Hille family numbered eight. Two children had died: Michael, in childhood, and John, Jr., when he was thirty. The curse claimed its first victim in 1898. Magdalena Hille had been ill and a doctor was called. No one knows precisely what happened, but somehow the family physician mistakenly gave Mrs. Hille a fatal dose of poison. A short time later John Hille, the immigrant who had turned a Wisconsin forest into thriving farmland, died at nearly ninety years of age. His death was attributed to natural causes. Shortly thereafter a son, who had been an invalid for some time, followed his parents and two brothers in death.

The family which had been eight was now five.

Two sons, Oscar and William, and a sister, Hulda, inherited the large estate. Several other children had moved away and showed no interest in farming. By all accounts, the trio that remained on the farm was well respected by their neighbors and thrifty in their financial affairs, making the farm one of the most profitable in the county.

Nearly a decade passed before tragedy again struck the Hille family.

Oscar Hille died in 1916. He had taken a bull to a water trough early one morning. The animal had been led back to its stall and tethered to a post when it suddenly bolted and crushed Oscar against a wall. He died two days later of internal injuries.

Strangest of all the deaths attributed to the curse was the macabre scenario played out at the Hille farm two years after Oscar's death.

The war in Europe had reached into America's midlands as young men marched off to battle the Kaiser. At home, sewing circles formed to make warm woolen clothing for the forces overseas, the Red Cross and YMCA asked for donations, and the purchase of Liberty Bonds and War Stamps was a strong measure of patriotism.

William and Hulda were particularly touched by the war. Both their parents had been born in the land now being torn asunder by battle. They had many Old World customs, and their hearts must have ached at the suffering and loss on both sides. William didn't like to discuss the war. "It's useless to argue," he often said. His reticence to talk about the war, and his Germanic background, may have led some of his neighbors to suspect him of disloyalty, although members of his family later convincingly rebutted such speculation. The suspicions stalked William and Hulda with tragic consequences.

The morning of July 11, 1918, broke gently over the lazily moving Fox River a few hundred yards behind the Hille house. The couple went about their chores as they did each day, but there was a tenseness about them, almost as if their world would soon crumble. Several weeks earlier, a man named Elder Krause had ingratiated himself with the Hilles and persuaded them to take him on as a hired man. Krause told his new employers that he was from South Milwaukee. But after several days his behavior changed abruptly. Krause said he was actually an "agent" of the U.S. Secret Service and was there because of reports that the couple were disloyal. It soon became apparent that the story was false and Krause's actual purpose was to extort money from William and Hulda. He enlisted the aid of a neighbor boy, Ernest Fentz, who performed odd jobs for William. Newspaper accounts of the day say Krause and Fentz threatened the Hilles with "exposure" as disloyal Americans unless they acquiesced to their demands.

There is little, if any, evidence that either William or Hulda was disloyal; on the contrary, they gave generously to the war effort. But a packet of letters found later in the Hille farmhouse indicated something mysterious and sinister in Krause's ways. One note from Hulda alluded to some past misdeed that was so bad that she had torn up the letter Krause sent threatening her with its exposure.

Fentz's role in the blackmail is unclear. William Hille had always liked the boy, buying him gifts and often allowing him to ride in a car Hille had recently purchased. Hille turned against the boy when he teamed up with Krause in the blackmail scheme. Fentz was fired from his job at the Hille farm in late June and told never to return.

The climax to this peculiar chain of events took place shortly before noon on July 11. Elder Krause stopped by the home of young Fentz, saying he wanted him to come along to the Hille farm because he "had a good position for him." The lad's father tried to persuade his stepson not to go, but Fentz wouldn't listen and left with Krause.

At the farm, William apparently relented and gave Krause and Fentz thirty dollars for "protection against exposure." Fentz handed Hille a crudely drawn receipt for the money. It is not known what information would be "exposed" or from whom the Hilles would be safe. Krause, Fentz, and William then fell to arguing. Hulda Hille, who was deeply fearful that the pair was "after them," telephoned a neighbor, Mrs. William Dingeldine, and asked her to hurry over. The woman had just arrived at the kitchen door when a sharp explosion reverberated from the direction of the living room. Seconds later William walked into the kitchen holding a shotgun. When he saw Mrs. Dingeldine he offered to shake hands, but instead she tried to grab the gun. Hulda stopped her neighbor. "Let him go," she said. "It is for the best. They're after us anyway, and you cannot prevent this. We will be dead before anyone can get here."

Ernest Fentz was already dead. His body lay slumped in a rocking chair in the living room, the left side of his face blown away by William's shotgun.

Hille pushed past Mrs. Dingeldine and started for the barn. She tried to reason with him, but he brushed her aside, echoing his sister's grim prediction: "They are after me," he said.

Hulda then handed a small wooden box to her neighbor and told her to leave. Hulda said there were valuable papers in the container and feared that Krause, who was still somewhere on the farm, might find them if he searched the house. Mrs. Dingeldine ran toward the road and home to telephone neighbors for help. When she reached the gate, shotgun blasts came from the direction of a barn. At about the same time she also heard Hulda yelling at Krause to "stay away from here." Krause had apparently heard the sound of gunfire and come to investigate. After the woman's warning he fled across a nearby field.

At the Hille farm a slaughter had begun. William had methodically killed five horses with shots fired into their heads. Back in the kitchen, he then shot and killed a pet dog. Hulda, too, heard the shooting as she lay in bed upstairs, an empty bottle of arsenic and a razor blade next to her on a table. The poison would act swiftly enough, she decided, as life drained from her body. The last sound she heard was her brother climbing the stairs and entering his bedroom. He sat in a favorite chair and balanced the shotgun against his legs, its barrel pointing directly at his midsection. Against the trigger was the tip of a long, thin strip of wood. That would be his remote triggering device when the time came. He looked for one last time out the window to his beloved farm and remembered that it was the land his father and mother had wrested from a savage wilderness and made thrive. Now he was an old man, and "they" were after him. The crashing roar of the gun shattered the stillness. William's upper torso was ripped away. Down the hall, his sister also lay dead.

One man murdered, two people dead by their own hands, and six farm animals slaughtered. Why? What motivated this orgy of violence? A coroner's inquest and the recollections of the three surviving Hille sisters tried to shed some light on the tragedy.

The sisters argued that their brother and sister were "loyal American citizens." They said Elder Krause's only object in coming to work for William and Hulda had been to get money from them on one pretext or another, and when he could not persuade them in any way he made threats by posing as a "secret service man." William gave Krause the thirty dollars, hoping to be rid of him. When Krause and Fentz didn't seem satisfied and William threatened to call the authorities, an argument took place that led to the deaths.

The coroner's inquest left many questions unanswered. Krause was finally located in St. Paul,

Minnesota, trying to enlist in the army. Waukesha authorities were said to have gone after Krause to bring him back, but his testimony was not included in the coroner's report.

The most mysterious aspect of the inquest dealt with a letter found in the box given to Mrs. Dingeldine by Hulda Hille. In the note, Hulda predicted her own death!

It read: "Say girls, the other night there was a slapping noise on the wall. I knew what that meant, so good-bye. All be good with Eliza. There are only these three left. We will try our best to get our rights. Don't take it hard, because Bill would have to be in prison for life; he [Krause] was telling Bill about the Japs [sic] coming over and how they will come. And then Bill—we would go in the house and shoot them. Give the machine to H. and A. That is W's wish."

On the opposite side of the sheet of paper Hulda listed the pallbearers she wanted at her funeral.

What crime had William committed that would be punishable by life imprisonment? How did Hulda know in advance that their deaths were imminent? Was the slapping noise an omen? The questions cannot be satisfactorily answered. We can only surmise that the harassment of the elderly couple by Krause and Fentz had caused an initial consternation that became fear and paranoia. William and Hulda were convinced that some unspoken past deed or utterance would cause their arrest and imprisonment. Sadly, there is little evidence to support their fears. They were trapped by the diabolical pretenses of Elder Krause and Ernest Fentz . . . and the Hille curse.

The farm reverted to Mrs. Jacob Hahn of Delafield, Wisconsin, one of the three surviving sisters. Over the next decades a cloud of disaster has hung over all those who live in the great old stone farmhouse.

Mrs. Hahn sold the farm in late 1918 to H. A. Kuhtz. The Kuhtz family built a milkhouse and enlarged the barn. But Kuhtz went bankrupt in 1927 and Mrs. Hahn took the farm back.

From 1927 until 1929, a young couple whose names have been lost to history rented the house. They too suffered from the Hille curse. Two of their children died of the baffling crib death.

After 1929 no one lived on the farm for nearly twenty years, but that didn't prevent the curse from working its evil. In 1932 a man named Pratt was killed while dynamiting stone in a farm pasture.

On a clear, bright, beautiful morning in September 1948, Mr. and Mrs. Ralph Ransome first saw the stone house standing abandoned amid weeds and bittersweet as the couple drove slowly down River Road. The Ransomes owned several health spas in Chicago and were looking for property to which they might retire someday. As Dorothy Ransome gazed at the house sitting way back in a grove of thirteen massive oak trees, she knew it was the house for her. They proceeded to walk around the yard and peer into the dimly lit rooms through dust-encrusted windows. Mrs. Ransome was determined to find the owner. Incredibly, the house was still in the possession of Mrs. Jacob Hahn, the last surviving Hille sister. The octogenarian agreed to sell the house only after the Ransomes promised to restore the home to its original splendor.

Various architects said it would be extraordinarily expensive to restore the house, but Dorothy Ransome insisted that it be saved since she had made that promise to Mrs. Hahn.

Work on the restoration began in 1948 and was completed four years later. The roof was removed and the interior of the house was torn out and rebuilt. The only part of the house to remain intact was the eighteen-inch-thick fieldstone walls. The Ransomes lavished vast sums on the house's rebirth. Stained glass from an old funeral home was fitted into several windows; a marble fireplace, which had been the centerpiece of a New Orleans mansion, went into the living room. Crystal chandeliers from the old McCormick mansion in Chicago were wired into the dining room and parlor. Finally, the house stood proud and beautiful, surrounded by spacious lawns and clipped

"Ravensholme"

hedges.

In 1953, Anita Ransome, their only daughter, met and married young Andrew Kennedy while they were both students at Northwestern University. The couple moved to the farm that same year, while the Ransomes continued their business obligations in Chicago.

Meanwhile, they began to hear about the tragedies connected with the old farm. Neighbors warned them that terrible things happened to anyone who lived at the old Hille house. Tear it down, the neighbors told them, or dynamite it, but don't live on that farm! The Ransomes were to learn they were not immune to the legacy.

The first calamity in the Ransome family was not, however, directly connected with the farm. Their grandson, seven-year-old Philip Kennedy, drowned in 1963 while swimming in Lake Mendota, in Madison, during a family outing. Nine years later the farm would claim its most recent victim. Ralph and Dorothy Ransome had retired in 1971 and moved to the farm they called Ravensholme, adapted from the original English spelling of Ralph Ransome's last name. Their daughter and son-in-law had separated. Five-year-old Ransome Kennedy was living with his grandparents on the farm, enjoying the delights and distractions a young boy can find in the country. But, on March 17, 1972, while young Ransome was playing in the barn he fell into an auger and was crushed to death. The curse had struck again.

Dorothy Ransome first saw the ghost during the summer of 1972. On several occasions she would be sitting at the kitchen table stringing beans or reading, when a furtive, fleeting shadow, the figure of a man, would slip across the back yard and come toward the kitchen door.

When she reached the door no one was ever there.

"At first I thought it was a shadow," Mrs. Ransome says. "But this has persisted. He comes across the back, although I have seen him out on the driveway. It's old John Hille. He's got an old black coat on, a crouched hat, and walks quite fast but he's old. And his coat is way up in back and hangs in the front. Each time I see him he comes to the kitchen door." That was the door John Hille always used.

Dorothy Ransome isn't afraid of the ghost at all. She thinks he is happy and pleased that his farm has been well cared for. He appears at different times of the day and never at night. He is always moving very quickly with his arms swinging at his sides as if he is in a hurry.

When Mrs. Ransome sees the ghost and goes to the back door, her cat will often suddenly sit up and stare at the door at the same instance the specter appears.

Why would John Hille haunt his old farm? Because, Dorothy Ransome reasons, he put his whole being into the farm. "He built this house with his own hands. Cleared all the land, too. His family was raised here. I think he loved it so deeply and it meant so much to him that his spirit is still around. The neighbors are scared to death of this place. But I have nothing but love for it."

Mrs. Ransome cannot, however, understand the tragedies that have afflicted her home. "The neighbors still say there is a curse on this farm. We laughed at it at first, but there has been a constant stream of tragedies right straight through. It's always been the same."

Perhaps it always will be.

Part V.
Mysterious Milwaukee

GIDDINGS'S HAUNTED BOARDINGHOUSE

Nobody ran a boardinghouse with the aplomb of Mrs. William Giddings. She filled her South Side Milwaukee home with employees of the local tannery and catered to her men with calm efficiency. The two-story frame house, at the corner of Allis and Whitcomb streets in Allen's Addition, soon earned a reputation as a haven of solitude where nothing more disturbing than the death of a kitten ever occurred.

But that was before August 8, 1874. At nine o'clock on that Saturday morning, Giddings was at work at the rolling mill; his wife and Mary Spiegel, the hired girl, were alone in the house working in the kitchen. Mary, the daughter of a neighboring Polish family, was a slow-witted child whose father brutalized her so severely that she welcomed the opportunity to "hire out." Although living in a constant state of nervous apprehension, she was treated with compassion and charity by her employer.

The women were making pies for dinner when suddenly spoons leaped from their holder and flew in all directions around the room. Only momentarily startled, the older woman continued with her work—until a trap door in the kitchen floor began to rise and fall. Mrs. Giddings asked fourteen-year-old Mary to stand on it. When the youngster was unable to hold down the heaving door, the woman knew some prankster had gotten into the cellar. She lifted the door, descended, but saw no one.

Climbing back into the kitchen, she found everything in motion. Dishes flew from the china closet and smashed on the floor. An oil lamp soared from its shelf and shattered. Chairs rose to the ceiling and one broke upon hitting the floor. The stove danced. One of the pies fell from the table, a dish of beans spilled, and eggs whirled out of the pantry that was open to the kitchen. One egg, following a trajectory, cut across a corner to hit Mrs. Giddings where she sat.

Mary, greatly frightened, was sent to get the neighbors, Mrs. Mead and Mrs. Rowland, to come sit with them. As the women approached Giddings's house, a pail of flowers at the door leaped over the five-and-a-half-foot wooden fence into the next yard. It was brought back but again flew over the same fence.

Once inside, the four women sat in a circle. Mary began peeling potatoes for dinner. As she talked, the knife flew out of her hand, along with a potato from the pan in her lap; both hit Mrs. Rowland. In the next moment, a dish on the table cracked in two. None of the group was near enough to the table to have reached the dish. One piece fell to the floor; the other remained on the table. Corn, boiling on the stove, leaped out of its pot.

The resolute Mrs. Giddings tried to keep her composure. The next door neighbor, Mrs. Mead, lost hers. Visibly upset, she announced that she was going home. No sooner had she reached her own yard than a heavy stick of wood was hurled over the fence at her. Mary was at the far end of Giddings's yard and reportedly couldn't have lifted the stick anyway.

Pails of water also traveled over the fence and back again, and no more than one pail in four was spilled.

Curiosity soon brought throngs of neighbor women to the house and terror kept them there. Finally, the bewildered Mrs. Giddings sent Mary to get George W.

Allen and his brother, Rufus, owners of the Wisconsin Leather Company. The men were at their tannery near Giddings's home and they came promptly to the house, bringing with them a Dr. Meacham and Dr. Nathaniel A. Gray, an eminent Milwaukee obstetrician.

While George Allen tried to calm the women, a stove-lid lifter flew off the wood stove, hurtled ten feet through the air, and struck Allen on the leg. No one was closer to the stove than he. Then, a pie rose from the table, flew past him, and smashed against the stove. To avoid further bombardments, Allen left the room.

By this time the floor was littered with the debris of broken dishes, splintered wood, shards of glass, and spilled food. Mrs. Giddings asked Mary to sweep, and as she did so, Dr. Meacham kept a close, scrutinizing eye on her. From where he stood, he had a full view of the pantry and of the servant. As he watched, a small china dish sailed horizontally out of the pantry. He dodged it and it slid to the floor, spilling the cards it contained, but not breaking.

Mary then began to wash the floor, but the pail of soapy water skated to the outer edges of the room, into the crowd of frightened onlookers. As Mary got off her knees to chase the pail, she was hit hard on the head by a bowl flying out of the pantry. The men searched the pantry, the kitchen, and the dining room but found no devices that might have propelled objects into space.

The manifestations continued until late afternoon. By that time, reporters from the local press had arrived to interview the men and all the women still present. They questioned each eyewitness independently and were completely satisfied that there had been no collusion. Since the phenomena occurred only in Mary's presence, there was some speculation that she might have thrown some of the objects. But the scrupulous observations made by the witnesses and the unnatural ballistics of the moving objects exonerated the girl. That the phenomena had indeed occurred without human agency was vouched for by literally scores of eyewitnesses who were highly regarded and generally considered to be beyond impeachment.

One reporter also had a talk with Mary. He found her to be a pitiable creature fearful of staying in the house or of doing anything. She could not explain how the manifestations had occurred, and she denied all responsibility for them. The reporter also learned that the child sometimes got up in the night to fight imaginary enemies. Mrs. Spiegel, who was present during the interview and who spoke no English, thought that the note-taking newsman was a law enforcement officer gathering evidence to support a charge of witchcraft against her daughter. She scolded Mary repeatedly and the little girl huddled deep in her chair and trembled and cried.

Saturday evening, the Giddingses decided that they could not keep the girl and they told her to go home. She begged to stay and when her pleadings were of no avail she hid herself in the woodshed. Her father found her there and, in order to make amends, beat the child severely.

The next that was heard of Mary was her attempted suicide in the river. An unnamed gentleman rescued her, soaked and shivering, and took her to Giddings's house. When asked why she had tried to kill herself, she said she was so hounded by everybody that she could no longer endure her life.

Again her former employers sent her back to her parents, and the charitable Mrs. Giddings sent along a dish of food. The next day Mary returned the empty dish. No sooner had she put it on the kitchen table than the tea kettle leaped off the stove, hit the floor, and was damaged beyond repair. Giddings, hearing the commotion and fearing further destruction of his property, drove Mary out of the house.

Two days later she was taken back to the house by Dr. Chauncey C. Robinson, a prominent physician of the city who had taken an interest in the girl and wanted to question Mrs. Giddings about the strange phenomena. The family and the boarders were eating dinner; the moment that Mary and the doctor entered the room, knives and forks flew off the table.

According to news accounts, Mary was finally taken into the home of a well-known physician in the Seventh Ward.

Was Mary the focus of the upheaval? Parapsychologists believe that neurotic conditions are among the factors that conduce to poltergeist activity, and it was the consensus of the time that Mary was neurotic. Did her neurosis and somnambulism facilitate the unconscious release of paranormal powers? Or were the levitations the result of some natural phenomenon—the movement of underground water? A localized earthquake? Natural settling of the house? Mass hallucination?

Because all normal explanations seemed preposterous, the little servant girl attracted international attention. In *Ghosts and Poltergeists*, author Herbert Thurston, a Jesuit investigator of psychic phenomena, includes the story of Mary Spiegel. He calls it a "remarkable American case."

THE GHOST WHO SOUGHT REVENGE

In 1874, a black man was beaten to death in Milwaukee's Palmer's Addition. One evening shortly after his death, his ghost appeared on the street corner where the fatal brawl had occurred. Baleful eyes were fixed upon the faces of passers-by hurrying home from work—eyes that threatened revenge upon the murderers.

But few noticed the vaporous form loitering in the dim light. Caps were pulled low on foreheads, and coat collars were turned up against a raw wind blowing off the lake. Then two young fellows turned suddenly to cross the street. The ghost loomed large before them. One fellow swung a left hook that connected with empty air and sent him sprawling into the gutter. The other spun around and ducked into a corner tavern. Risking ridicule, both men reported what they had seen, and soon people came from all over the city to see the murdered man's ghost. Some were fascinated, some were repelled, and others were only mildly curious.

Night after night the apparition appeared on the street corner, its evil eyes staring from its pallid face. Gradually, from a sense of resignation and futility perhaps, the ghost's visits diminished until, four years later, it appeared infrequently and then only to a handful of loyal spectators. Insofar as is known, the ghost never found its slayer.

HOUSE OF EVIL

Violent death is often the catalyst for the appearance of a ghost. Those who die at the hands of a murderer or take their own lives are said to frequently leave behind strong energy impressions that may be manifested in the activity of a ghost or poltergeist.

Present-day Milwaukee residents passing the corner of Twelfth Street and State are unaware that they are within a few feet of the location of one of that city's most famous haunted houses. The brick house is gone now, but its sinister reputation persisted for many years. It belonged to Major Hobart. He left earth too soon and his house was never the same.

Hobart, a former army officer, calmly hanged himself for unexplained reasons one afternoon. He was found swinging from a chandelier in the large two-story home. After Hobart's demise, many families lived in the house, but few remained for more than several months. The terrified residents reported doors opening and closing without human assistance, footfalls clattering up the staircase when all were in bed, groans echoing from various rooms, and chains being dragged across the floors.

When the house was vacant, and that was frequently, neighbors would notice lights through the dusty windows, solidifying the house's reputation for evil.

After several years, no realtor could sell the

brick mansion, so infamous had its reputation become. At last it was razed, and with it were lost the last, unearthly traces of Major Hobart, late of the United States Army.

HOUSE OF MUFFLED SCREAMS

There is something about an old house that invites rumors of ghosts. Had a deceased occupant met a violent death within its walls? Been given an unsatisfactory burial? Or just hung around, as a curious specter, to keep an eye on things?

Motives for ghostly activities differ, but the residents of Milwaukee's Sixth Ward, back in 1875, didn't differ in their opinion of the unpainted frame house in their neighborhood. They knew it was haunted. The square two-story structure, one of the oldest in the city, stood high on the west bluff, overhanging the river, southeast of the reservoir. Its windows offered a splendid view of the city, and the house itself, if not elegant, was spacious, containing a cellar, four rooms on the first floor, two large rooms and two closets on the second, and a garret. Yet, for all its amenities, no one ever lived there very long. Tenants came and went, and most told stories of seeing strange lights and hearing strange sounds.

After a Polish family moved out, in fear, Herman Hegner, who had the key to the house and was in charge of renting it, decided to make his own observations. He watched the house closely on the first night that it was vacant. Shortly after midnight, he saw the room in the southwest corner of the first floor suddenly fill with light. Fearing that the house was on fire, he raced out his door and up to the window where the light shone, but just before he reached it, the light disappeared. He groped in his pocket for the front door key, but before he could move from the window, the light shone again with blinding brilliance, then disappeared. Hegner put the key in the lock, pushed open the old door. It creaked on its hinges. The old man moved from room to room, peering into dark corners and musty closets. There was no living thing anywhere. Hegner was perplexed. Although unable to explain the light, he was certain it was not produced by human agency.

In July 1875, new immigrants, a Bohemian family of five, moved into the house. Weary from their long journey, they settled down for the night on the first floor and fell asleep promptly. Suddenly the parents were awakened. Heavy footsteps tramped the floor above. A muffled scream trembled in the air, and then the resounding crash of a body falling to the floor shook the walls of the old building. The restless children stirred but did not awaken.

On the second night, the sequence of events was repeated, with increased violence. And at one o'clock in the morning, the terror-stricken family fled to Hegner's house. At dawn they gathered up their possessions and left the area.

On Sunday night, August 8, 1875, two resident Englishmen, George E. Heath and Henry Jordan, asked the caretaker for permission to spend that night in the house to either expose the delusion or capture the ghost. Heath, a blacksmith, and Jordan, a close friend, worked in the Milwaukee and St. Paul railroad car shops and were considered responsible and trustworthy men.

Hegner gave them the key and a blanket apiece, and they went in. Piles of crumbled plaster lay on the floor; the bare walls were streaked with water stains where rain had dripped through the leaky roof; the kitchen floor was worn through in several places; and the old-fashioned stepladder leading to the garret was laced with cobwebs.

Early the next morning, Hegner went to the house and found the front door wide open, his blankets lying in one of the downstairs rooms, and the visitors gone. What had happened?

A newsman sought out George Heath. Heath said that he and Jordan had checked the house just after sunset to make sure that no one was hiding inside. Finding no living thing, not even a rat, they walked down to the roundhouse where they stayed until after ten o'clock. Then they walked back up the hill to the house and sat around smoking until they got tired enough to sleep.

Heath went on, "I was awakened by Jordan, who told me he had heard some noise upstairs. We sat up for a moment and then heard someone walking stealthily across the floor above; then there was a pause followed by a noise as of someone leaping on the floor. A scuffle followed, I heard a smothered cry and a heavy fall, and then all was still. I proposed to go upstairs, and was just about to strike a match with which to light our candle when the room we were in was filled with a blinding light.

For a moment my eyes were dazzled so that I could distinguish nothing; then I saw Jordan point toward the stairway visible through the open room door. I looked, but saw nothing.

"The light seemed to last for about a minute

and then went out. It might have been longer, or shorter, I cannot certainly say. I lit the candle and looked at my watch. It was twenty-five minutes past twelve. I was not frightened in the least, and insisted upon going upstairs; at first Jordan hesitated, but when I moved he followed me. We searched both rooms and closets, but found no trace of anything, living or dead."

The men also climbed the ladder and searched the garret, but nothing was there. Going back downstairs, they decided to stay awake and watch. They blew out their candle and sat silently, waiting. In about fifteen minutes the stealthy footsteps sounded. Then the brief pause, the leap, the muffled cry, struggle, and fall. And when it was over, the light filled the room as before. Heath wanted to search again, but Jordan refused to spend another minute in the house, so both men left.

When Heath was asked if he had an explanation for the strange phenomena, he could give none. He said only that he did not believe that ghosts had anything to do with it.

If it wasn't ghosts, what was it?

THE FACE ON THE BEDROOM CURTAIN

Early on Saturday morning, September 21, 1878, Milwaukee resident Mary Tubey died. Although the circumstances of her death were not unusual, her youth made her passing especially poignant to her relatives.

A block away, on Hill Street between Seventh and Eighth, her stepbrother, Dan Connell, had finished his noon dinner and was sitting in the front room, silent and alone with his grief. The door to the bedroom was open, and from where he sat he had a clear view of the window in that room. Suddenly he saw Mary's face on the curtain. Was it just a shadow? A pattern created by the folds of the material? No, the longer he looked, the clearer the face became.

Connell called his wife, and she too saw the strange likeness. They tried to divert their uneasiness by keeping busy in the house, but their curiosity impelled them to check the curtain several times during the afternoon. The face was always there . . . shimmering, smiling . . . in exactly the same place. Had Mary returned to say good-bye, or were the Connells, in their sorrow, imagining her presence?

Later that day the story got out, and neighbors by the dozens swarmed through the front and back doors of the small brown cottage. Some glanced at the curtain and, seeing nothing, held their laughter until they got outdoors; others were profoundly moved by what they believed they saw. A policeman, who visited the house at three o'clock, said later that he had never seen anything plainer in his life.

When the size of the crowds became unmanageable and the Connells were chilled to the bone from the cold air blowing through the open doorways, they barricaded the entrances and refused to admit more visitors.

The next day, Sunday, the crowds swelled into the hundreds. The doors were opened again and the curious callers filed past the window curtain. At dusk the phantom vanished but the visitors did not. From all parts of the city they came, and many were deeply disappointed upon learning that there was no longer anything to be seen.

The following week, a local reporter called on Mrs. Connell and also interviewed a number of neighbors who claimed to have seen the apparition. Each was positive that he had seen the face on the curtain. Some said emphatically that they could not be deceived, and all cross-questioning failed to shake them. They were so solemn about the affair that the reporter decided it was folly to hint that they were victims of imagination.

Were they?

THE GHOST OF GRAND AVENUE

Mr. Jones, a black man, was married to a white woman. In about 1880, the couple lived in a cottage in Merrill Park near the end of Milwaukee's Grand Avenue. But Mrs. Jones's brothers, who hated their brother-in-law, eventually murdered him. Thereafter, his ghost, on a large white horse, rode up and down the avenue late at night, frightening everyone who saw it.

THE GHOST KNOCKS ONCE

Mr. White was a Sunday School teacher at St. James Church in Milwaukee many years ago. He often told friends of a ghostly experience he had had some time before.

White was sitting in his home when he heard a knock at the door. He opened it. On the threshold stood a vague human form he recognized as a woman friend who lived many miles away. Before White could speak she faded away.

The gentle schoolteacher learned a few days later that the woman had died at nearly the precise moment he had seen her on his front porch.

THE VEILED LADIES

In the early 1900s, Mrs. Schwassman and other Milwaukee residents saw, at twilight, a procession of veiled white women floating silently not far above the ground.

THE RESTLESS SERVANT GIRL

In 1908, Dr. Gerhard Bading and his wife were living in a house they had rented on Milwaukee's west side, on Upper Wells Street between Twenty-fifth and Twenty-sixth streets. It was a large clapboard house with double stairways typical of the era. One staircase connected the front of the house to the upstairs hall and the other connected the rear portion of the upstairs hall to the kitchen. The hallway and both stairways were carpeted. That year, the Badings decided to take a short trip, and, not wishing to leave the house unattended, they asked their friend, Dr. E.J.W. Notz, to occupy the place in their absence.

Notz moved in on the appointed day and that night went upstairs to bed and fell promptly asleep.

Shortly after midnight he was awakened by a thundering crash followed by footsteps padding in the hallway. He sat up in bed, then thought he heard the footsteps going down the rear stairway. They were definitely footsteps. He was certain he was not alone in the house. He got up quickly, turned on lights, and searched the attic, second floor, first floor, basement. There was no one anywhere, nor could Notz find evidence of anything that might have caused the disturbance. Satisfied and much relieved, he went back to bed and fell asleep, until . . .

A sudden crash, then hurried footsteps across the hall and down the stairway awoke him again. He got up and searched the house for the invisible prowler. He found no one. Nothing had been disturbed.

The commotion erupted a third time before morning, and the same sequence occurred during Notz's second night in the house. Uneasy and thoroughly baffled by this time, he mentioned the matter to some relatives living in the city; they had no explanation either.

When the Badings returned, Notz told them of his experiences, but they showed no surprise. They said they had heard those noises so often that they weren't greatly disturbed by them.

Later, Notz learned that people in the neighborhood believed the house was haunted by the ghost of a servant girl who had committed suicide on the premises. She had been sent to the house early one fall day to open it up and get it ready for its owner, the proprietor of a resort hotel in the Waukesha Lakes area. The girl was apparently suffering from depression and, once in the house, was unable to complete her work. After her death, her restless ghost roamed the hall and stairways, frightening every family who ever lived there.

The Legacy of Mary Buth Farm

The weather was warm for December 31. Wispy strands of fog clung to the gently rolling fields of southeastern Wisconsin as the thermometer hovered near thirty degrees. At the end of a long paved road near Germantown, the Tom Walton family prepared to celebrate New Year's Day, 1966, in their 140-year-old farmhouse. Somewhere a clock struck midnight. Family members and several guests toasted each other for success and happiness in the coming twelve months.

The main house at Mary Buth farm

But, according to what Walton later told a news reporter, the evening had not been cheerful. There was a tinge of something sinister, something almost evil intruding upon the celebration. Walton, a professor of education at the University of Wisconsin-Milwaukee, remembered that night. "The whole evening was strange. Small things happened at first. The house suddenly cooled for no apparent reason. A candle burned much faster than its twin sitting nearby. The television set lost power—again without explanation. And then, outside the wide living room window, *she* appeared. An old woman, dressed in a rough black dress, stared in at the assembled family and guests. Before Walton could act, she was gone.

Who was *she* . . . that vague, dark phantom staring in at the startled assemblage? Walton had a hunch—a hunch that led back in time to 1838.

In that year, John and Mary Buth built the farm as one of Wisconsin's pioneer homesteads. In its early days, the Buth cabin and land were used as a trading post for early settlers and traders. Near the farm, Indians camped near a small stream. The decades have brought innumerable changes to the original house, but a section of the original log cabin forms a part of the present two-story frame house. Sturdy log ceiling beams now support part of the second floor. The place is still known as Mary Buth Farm.

John and Mary Buth had three children: Herman, who died at age seventy in 1917; Carl, who died at age seventy-four in 1923; and Mary, the only daughter and the farm's namesake, seventy-six at her death in 1926. None of the children married. A weed-shrouded cemetery near the farm holds their remains.

How does this explain the Waltons' eerie New Year's night? The Buth farm has a history of being haunted. The ghosts of Mary Buth and her mother were said to roam the farm by day and inhabit the house at night. Tom Walton had heard neighbors tell stories of peculiar events occurring in or near the Buth farm. Walton and his family moved to the farm in 1961 and didn't place much faith in the tales until that night in 1965.

On that evening Walton changed his mind. The fleeting apparition outside the window left him perplexed. The next morning he discovered that a pepper plant near the window had wilted leaves on one side while the other half remained green and healthy. The other small incidents that night added to the mystery.

Over the next months and years, until 1976 when the family moved away, the Waltons were to have other baffling experiences. An overnight visitor told Walton that he had seen in the yard a young girl who vanished into the early morning mist. The Buth farm is quite isolated from nearby houses.

One afternoon, Walton was alone in the house when the clear, distinct notes of a violin floated through the house. No radio was playing. The stereo was turned off. The violin music alone echoed through the silent rooms. Later, Walton learned that Herman Buth had played violin as a hobby.

On another occasion, when the kitchen was being remodeled, the Waltons' plumber said he had heard footsteps walking across the upstairs floor. The plumber had been alone in the house at the time.

What caused these incidents? To find out, Walton asked a psychic and writer, Mary Leader, to visit the home. After a session with a Ouija board, Mrs. Leader said at least two ghosts haunted the Buth farm. She identified them as Mary Buth (the mother) and her daughter, Mary. Mrs. Leader said the daughter was an evil ghost lurking outside the home and searching for her missing lover. According to local lore, Mary had been left standing at the altar on her wedding day. The mother was the "inside" ghost protecting the house from her daughter. Mrs. Leader could not explain the violin music Walton had heard.

Some neighbors scoff at the idea of *either* Mary coming back to haunt the house. One resident said several years ago, "She [Mary, the younger] just wasn't the type who would come around and haunt [the farm]. Sure she was an old maid and probably a little eccentric, but she had a good heart." Mary reportedly cared for the mentally retarded people in the vicinity during an era when they were shunned by most of society.

Few contemporary accounts remain of the elder Mary. She was ninety-three at her death in 1899, outliving her husband by forty-six years.

Nearly everyone agrees that young Mary and her brothers were hard-working farmers who cut wood with a handsaw and offered the use of their farm as a resting place for peddlers traveling from Milwaukee. Is it possible that one of these itinerant salesmen proposed to Mary and then jilted her when a new territory beckoned? It has been known to happen.

A former resident of the farm, whose family lived in the house from 1945 to 1954, says he never saw a ghost there. But, he says, a coven of witches did want to buy the farm at one time.

The John Ewens family moved to the Buth farm in 1976. They, too, have been told the ghost stories. Ewens said neighborhood children believe the house is haunted and are reluctant to visit it.

Do the spirits of Mary Buth, mother and daughter, haunt the ancient structure? Is Herman Buth still fiddling at the house he lived in all his life? Tom Walton still can't explain the strange things that happend on that New Year's Eve in 1965. As far as he is concerned, the ghosts were very much a part of his family's life at Mary Buth Farm.

TERROR IN THE NIGHT

March 18, 1975. Darkness wrapped the old-fashioned, clapboard farmhouse near Cedarburg. Upstairs, Barb Yashinsky lay sleeping. It had been a long, exhausting day moving the family into their new home. At two o'clock in the morning, Barb was awakened by a crying noise. "I thought it was a cat fight," she recalls, "and you know what they sound like."

Wide awake and listening intently, she decided the sounds were more like those of a crying child. Had Kate awakened and become frightened by her strange surroundings? Barb got up, crossed the hall, and opened the door to her daughter's bedroom. The little girl was sound asleep.

Then Barb thought she heard a woman's voice scolding the child. More curious than frightened, she went downstairs and toured the house. Everything seemed in order. She went outdoors and searched the grounds but found nothing to account for the disturbance.

She returned to bed; the crying persisted. It seemed now to be coming from the closet area of the bedroom, yet the woman's words were unintelligible, muffled, as if spoken from a distance. Was it just a peculiarity of the house? Of the neighborhood? Barb did not know, but she reasoned that unfamiliar houses, especially old ones, are often filled with creaks and groans to which one grows accustomed.

Twenty minutes after the crying had started, it subsided, and Barb drifted into sleep. Her husband, Michael, had never awakened and in the morning she decided not to mention the matter to him.

There was still much to do to convert the one-hundred-year-old house into a comfortable and cheerful home and Barb was eager to start. The previous owner, Jake Miller,* whose business was buying rundown houses and remodeling them for resale, had made only minimal, cosmetic changes before Yashinskys bought the place "for a song." It had stood empty for a year. Barb and Michael had had new wiring and central heating installed before they moved in, but now there was a great deal of painting to be done outside and inside. It would be a busy spring and summer. Barb had planned to return to full-time teaching that fall and was most anxious to complete the work on the house before then.

But the long, hard days of painting did not bring the anticipated satisfactions. Although neighbors admired the improvements and commented on how glad they were to see lights again in the old house, Barb was not enthused. She grew unaccountably nervous and restless. "I was never satisfied with anything," she explains, "which isn't like me. I couldn't find enough to keep me occupied. What I was doing was boring. I found lots of reasons to yell at the baby for no reason at all, but I thought I just needed to get back to work."

Barb's family noticed a definite personality change, a change that particularly disturbed Barb's mother, Margaret. The two women were very close.

By fall, much of the necessary work on the house had been finished and Barb returned to the classroom. Michael, a restaurant cook who works nights, cared for Kate during the daytime hours, and Margaret filled in for an hour or so on days when her daughter was unable to get home before Michael had to leave. Margaret also baby-sat during the evenings when Barb had a school function to attend. Yet the teaching didn't alleviate Barb's nervousness; she couldn't shake the apprehension that, at times, seemed to engulf her.

One night in November of 1975, Kate, who was two and one-half years old at that time, awoke with what her mother thought must be a nightmare. Hearing Kate's crying, Barb thought it odd; the child had always been a sound sleeper, never awakening in the middle of the night for any reason. Upon entering her daughter's room, Barb felt "the closing in of fear and apprehension which I was to experience many times." When she took Kate into her arms to comfort her, the child asked if the man would come again. Barb said he would not come, that she should go back to sleep. Although puzzled, Barb decided it was just a case of a small child with a large and vivid imagination.

The next night, Barb was awakened by Kate's screaming in utter terror. The child told her mother that the man had come again bringing animals that frightened her—circus animals. Barb's gentle chiding could not shake Kate's story; she was certain that a man had come and had brought animals into her room. According to her mother, Kate is a very bright and verbal child, yet she supplied no descriptions of the man or the animals and Barb thought it best not to question. Insofar as Kate's parents know, this was the last time their daughter ever heard or saw anything. Barb says of the experience, "This left me with a lot of questions and a lot of fears."

The following night, Barb was asleep alone; she had left Michael downstairs watching television. Suddenly she was awakened by a stinging slap across her face and a deep male voice calling "Barbara!" Astonished that her husband had hit her, she flung an arm out to the opposite side of the bed. It was empty.

"I was frozen to the bed with a great fear," Barb says. "I do remember praying and then getting enough courage to move . . . I was real heavy you know and I couldn't get myself up and I always scoffed when you see heroines in movies who can't move. I thought it's silly—you can always do anything you want. Your will is stronger. I was very, very scared."

But she did find her way downstairs to confront Michael. He was stunned; he had never left his seat by the television set! Who or what had struck his wife in that dark bedroom?

Still shaken and perplexed by the incident, Michael says, "I'll tell you, Barbara isn't the type to dream. That's why I couldn't figure it out. I'm a very logical individual. I couldn't figure out the logic for something like that. Knowing Barb as I do, she never lies.

I've known her for ten or twelve years now and she's never lied to me. It just wasn't Barb."

Meanwhile, there were other manifestations in the house for which Michael's logical mind found no rational explanation. Intense cold often filled the kitchen, the upstairs hallway, and Kate's bedroom, which was over the kitchen. At first, the couple reasoned that cold air was pouring in around the poorly fitted windows. Michael had new windows installed and did extensive caulking, yet the cold prevailed, especially in Kate's room. The child often awoke complaining that "I'm so cold." With the thermostat set at eighty-five degrees and hot air pouring forth from the register in Kate's room, Michael could see his breath while standing in the room. In the hallway, the newly applied wallpaper kept peeling and no amount of glue or pressure could keep the paper sealed to the plaster.

In the spring of 1976, Michael awoke in the early morning hours. He thought an odor had awakened him, but he could not identify the smell; he was certain it wasn't smoke. He sat up in bed and saw "something like a vapor coming up under the bedroom door. Something like steam. A heavy, damp kind of thing, whitish like fog. And it was transparent, yet you could see the lines of where it started and where it stopped. It was definitely a line surrounding the bottom of the door. It was subsiding as I looked at it, going down back under the door as I was seeing it."

Michael moved closer to Barb and asked her if she smelled anything. But she was sound asleep and when her husband looked back toward the closed door, the vapor was gone. Barb awoke too late to see the phenomenon, but she did get up to check Kate. Could it have been Michael's imagination? A reflection of light through the one bedroom window? Michael says, "Absolutely not. It wasn't light out. And the smell was what woke me up, but I can't remember what the odor was. The time it took to wake up from the smell and look and draw Barb's attention to it was a minute or two."

Sometime later, Michael was again awakened to find a blanket of fog surrounding the bed. "It reminded me of a screen completely encompassing the bed," he recalls. "You could look through it. But this time it had no odor." He did not awaken his wife this time nor did he get up to check the house, explaining that "I felt more secure if I just stayed where I was at."

Michael's experiences greatly upset Barb. "The next months left me fighting a great battle to remain calm in the evening hours," she says, "because we didn't seem to notice anything during the day. And so I'd have trouble. I rarely, if ever, went to bed without Mike. I'd sleep on the sofa until he'd come home and I'd check Kate a great many times."

In the fall of 1976 when Barb was preparing to return to teaching, her mother approached her one day and, in her customary straightforward manner, asked her daughter if she thought there might be something wrong with the house. Margaret complained that the kitchen was often so bitterly cold that she had to put on a sweater while working or doing crossword puzzles. At the same time, the adjoining living room and dining room were warm. Barb says that her mother is a very warm-blooded person, "usually wearing sleeveless when everyone else is wearing wool."

Now, her mother's feelings about the house

brought Barb some relief; she took comfort in the knowledge that she alone was not going crazy. Something unearthly, inexplicable must be in the house. Until that time, Barb and Michael had kept their strange experiences to themselves, questioning and probing for answers. Neither one subscribed to a belief in psychic phenomena; they had no interest in the subject nor had they had previous experiences that seemed to defy natural explanations.

Margaret suggested that her daughter and son-in-law have the house blessed, but Barb was afraid to have that done. "This person or whatever it is isn't aggressive or violent," she told her mother, "and who knows why it is here?" The house was never blessed.

In early January of 1977, Michael witnessed the last physical manifestation he was to see. He had been playing downstairs with Kate, and when it was her bedtime, he carried her upstairs, her head snuggled against his shoulder. Familiar with the stairway and house layout, he didn't bother to turn on lights. When he opened the door to his daughter's room, he stopped. There before him was a misty shape—a short, squat, figurelike form. It had no visible arms or legs, yet Michael sensed that it was "possibly a man. A man I felt more than saw as a man. It had definite lines to it. It was there. The lines of it were moving, vibrating. I've never seen anything like it. It wasn't something I could walk through so I stopped. You could see somewhat through it but nowhere near like the one that encompassed the bed. Then I reached over, turned on the light, and it was gone. It was extremely overcoming to me." Michael also noted that the cold was intense in the room.

Nevertheless, he put Kate to bed and he did not tell his wife of his experience at the time. Realizing that Barb was becoming more and more anxious, he didn't want to say anything that would increase her fears.

There was only one other strange experience in the house and that involved the family dog, a massive Great Pyrenees named Benjamin who slept each night in the master bedroom. Bennie had been sleeping on the floor at the foot of the bed, and Barb was sitting on the edge of the mattress in front of him. Michael was sitting on one side of the bed, and the two were talking in the dark.

Suddenly Bennie leaped to his feet, looked at Barb, and growled. Barb remembers being momentarily frightened, thinking the dog "had gone nuts or something" and was about to attack her. Then, in one great leap, he bounded past her and into the corner of the room, facing the closet where Barb had heard the crying child on the night the family had moved into the house. Bennie stood there growling for a moment, then, looking as if he had made a fool of himself, returned to his mistress to be hugged and patted.

That was the only time there had been a reaction from the animal. Both Barb and her husband had heard nothing. They claimed that Bennie could not have seen a mouse or any moving thing. The room was in total darkness and there was no light coming through the window because that window faced the dark back yard.

On January 13, 1977, the family moved out of the house. Michael says, "We just wanted to get out of there because we thought something might develop. The thing, whatever it was, seemed more and more disturbed that we were there." Barb says that although she never felt threatened by the thing, she wondered if it was going to change, "if it might start throwing pots and pans, rumpling bedding, or become hostile in some way." That was her real fear. She couldn't know whether the ghosts were aggravated by the presence of this new family in the house or whether they were merely curious. "It's silly to talk about it like this," she admits, "but you wonder. If Katie saw a man bringing animals maybe he was just interested in her as a child."

In their attempts to understand these experiences, the Yashinskys tried to learn something of the history of the house. They discovered that the place had been the original home of one of the area's farmers and that it had remained in the possession of this same family, except for a brief period when it had been sold to an outsider who never lived in the house. Yashinskys were the first outsiders ever to live in the place.

The last male member of the original family, Oliver Holcombe,* a reclusive bachelor, had died in the house and it had then passed to his widowed sister-in-law, Carrie Holcombe.* She lived in the house behind that had been built in the 1930s by her husband, Wilfred.* Neighbors said that Oliver never saw anyone but Carrie; they also reported that he had closed off the upstairs of the house because he had had no need of the space.

Carrie and her married son, Len,* provided more colorful information. According to family legend, a miserly ancestor was thought to have hidden a fortune in old coins somewhere in the house. If Len discounted the story, he was nevertheless sufficiently interested to have knocked out walls in a previous remodeling job to search for the coins himself. He told Michael the legend and recounted his own search for the money. Len himself had never lived in the house.

Although Barb had visited Carrie Holcombe a few times, she hadn't remembered ever seeing pictures of the Holcombe men in Carrie's home. After Michael's experience with the mist that he had sensed was a short, squat, malelike figure, Barb determined to find out what the Holcombe men looked like. She was able to contact Wilfred Holcombe's brothers, and she says, "They were short, stocky, broad-shouldered men."

Was the vapor that Michael had seen the ghost of Oliver who had died in the house? Or was it the ghost of the unknown ancestor who had secreted the coins? Which one was it? Were there two ghosts, both searching for the money? But who was the crying child? The scolding mother? An old house holds the secrets of the years, of births, of deaths, of distant tragedies. Had Jake Miller had an uncanny experience while working on the house? Is that why he quit work and unloaded the place at a low price?

Questions without answers. Barb and Michael figured that the treasure, if in fact it existed, was probably hidden somewhere in the walls of Kate's room and that was why the cold was centered basically in the kitchen and in the child's room, which shared a common wall. The creation of thought patterns, or ghosts, is said to draw energy from the surrounding atmosphere, which might explain why people feel extreme cold in areas where apparitions appear.

When the Yashinskys moved out, they told their story to the next-door neighbors, the Bartons,* whose daughter, Debbie,* had often baby-sat for them. Debbie always put all the lights on but Barb said nothing to her. She herself turned on all the lights when Michael was gone. "It was a comfort device," she says. "With the lights on I could at least see."

The Bartons said they had never heard any stories of supernatural phenomena connected with the house, but Mr. Barton refused to let Yashinskys talk to Debbie about it because he said she was a very emotional girl.

Later, Barb and Michael heard that Carrie claimed to have seen her deceased husband one day in the yard. Barb discounted the report, however, feeling that Carrie was very lonely, lived completely in the past, and was probably imagining things.

Could there be natural explanations for the Yashinskys' experiences that they may have overlooked? "No way," says Michael. "I'm a very logical person and . . . no way. It's gone over and over in my mind many times. I'm not an extremely well-read person, but I know what I know and I know what I saw, and nothing will ever change that. I was in a normal state. There was nothing physically or mentally wrong with me. I'm not a drinker. I don't take drugs. I'm very normal, so there's nothing illogical with me. Yet this happened to me, and knowing how Kate is, she saw what she saw."

Barb adds, "It's changed my ideas about people who I previously thought were crackpots for seeing ghosts or trying to film ghosts." She says she finally came to accept the supernatural basis for the phenomena because of the other witnesses to the manifestations. The experiences of her husband and her mother convinced her of the existence of things unknown, unknowable. Of her mother, Barb says, "She's the most stable person I have ever met; a very calm, quiet, sedate lady full of common sense and very much in control of her surroundings at all times. Her husband, too, worked nights so she spent a lot of time alone and she was never afraid."

The new house holds no terror in the night. And now when Kate wakes up each morning, she sighs and says, "Oh, Mama, it's so nice and warm in my room."

Meanwhile, Barb tries to put the past into perspective. "Although our experiences weren't particularly frightening, you just kind of want to forget." But then she adds a postscript, "We'll probably wrestle with this the rest of our lives."

Marie, The Caretaker Ghost

Remodeling a 120-year-old home can be a difficult chore under the best of circumstances. But two Milwaukee men have found the task is even more complicated when a resident ghost is in the house.

Paul Ranieri and Jeff Hicks had searched Milwaukee for nearly a year looking for just the right old house to which they could apply their restoration abilities. During the early summer of 1977 they found the house they wanted on National Avenue. It sat neglected between a large, rather undistinguished apartment building on one side and an industrial plant on the other. The brick dwelling had been scheduled for demolition, but the men could see its architectural and historical uniqueness and grew determined to purchase the house. After negotiation with the owners they bought it in August 1977.

The house had been unoccupied for nearly six months and a lack of upkeep had left it in a state of disrepair. Because of the condition of the house, it was clear the pair could not move in for some time. Cleaning out the accumulated debris would take weeks. But an attached apartment at the rear of the house was in good condition, and they decided to offer it for rent. The money would offset some of the costs of remodeling, and a renter could watch the property until Ranieri and Hicks moved in.

A few days later, Donald Erbs moved into the apartment. He would soon realize that someone or something was already living in the house.

For the first few days after Erbs moved in, his spare time was spent painting, refinishing some old furniture, and tending to his considerable collection of plants.

The first in a series of unexplainable events occurred about a week after he moved in. Erbs had finished a particularly long day at his job in the advertising department of a large photography store. He prepared a modest supper in his apartment, cleaned the dishes, and walked into his living room to listen to some music on his stereo.

Suddenly he noticed a young woman sitting in a chair directly across the room from him.

"I did not see her come in," Erbs recalls. "I don't know if she appeared or what, but all at once she was there."

Was he frightened? Not at first, Erbs says. He assumed "she" had some business being in the house and had come up the stairs to his living room.

Erbs's apartment is separated from the rest of the house by a long hallway with doors to his apartment, the main house, and one leading outside. His apartment is on two floors connected by a stairway.

As Erbs stared at the woman, he began to notice the strangeness of her appearance. It was very bright where she was sitting, Erbs says, "like she was giving off a light. As if somebody had a spotlight on her . . . almost overexposed and much brighter than her surroundings."

Her clothing, too, was peculiar. She was covered from neck to ankle in a dressing gown with fancy lacework at the neck and sleeves. He noted that her long, brown hair had a slight wave and her feet were bare.

Erbs began talking to her. What was her name, Erbs wanted to know. There was no answer. She continued to look directly at him with an almost dreamlike expression on her pale face. Erbs guessed she was about twenty years old.

After a few moments she began telling him about the house. Erbs says, "She told me a little about who built the house, which section had been built when, and why certain remodeling had been done. She told me the basement was originally the kitchen, and the dining room was at one time a restaurant."

The conversation, he says, was like one he would have with any "normal" person. But she was far from "normal."

At the end of her monologue the visitor stood up and walked out of the room. Erbs followed, but the mysterious woman vanished as suddenly as she had appeared. He could find no trace of her. The outside door remained locked, and there was no sound of retreating footsteps. Erbs estimates she was out of his sight for no longer than five seconds.

Although she appeared to be a solid human figure, there is no way she could have entered and left his apartment, or the house, in any natural way, Erbs says.

Who was Erbs's visitor?

"A ghost, or spirit," Erbs concludes. "Of that I am sure."

But what did she want? Who was she? And why had she picked Donald Erbs to talk with? The answers to some of these questions would come in the next few months.

Erbs told Ranieri and Hicks about his nocturnal visitor. They had given no one permission to be in the house and knew no one who matched the description Erbs provided. They were disturbed by the incident, but it did not alter their plans to move into the house in early October.

The next strange incident took place on the following Saturday.

Ranieri, Hicks, and Erbs were at work making various repairs in the house. Walls were stripped of yellowing wallpaper, floors prepared for refinishing, and various useless items accumulated in the house over the years tossed out.

Erbs had decided to install some shelving he had brought from a previous apartment. The job took over an hour, as the brackets for the shelves had to be anchored in the wall and the shelves secured to the protruding posts. He finished the job and left to join Hicks and Ranieri in another room.

Suddenly there was the sound of a crash from the room he had just left. The shelf had fallen to the floor, but a plant that Erbs had placed on the shelf was sitting undisturbed a few feet away. It was, Erbs says, as if someone had removed it from the shelf and placed it carefully on the floor.

Coincidence? Erbs had used the shelf in his previous home for several years without incident.

Neither Erbs nor his companions could explain it, but later that night an answer came in another visit from his mysterious guest.

It was late. Erbs sat alone in his apartment enjoying an old movie on television. Ranieri and Hicks had gone. There was no one else in the house . . . or so he thought.

Without warning the woman appeared in a chair next to him.

Startled, but less frightened than the first time, Erbs asked her if she had had anything to do with the shelf falling. Yes, she admitted. But it was not out of maliciousness. She had been looking at various items in the room and had accidentally knocked the shelf down.

Satisfied, Erbs again asked who she was. After a few seconds she answered, "Marie."

He then confidently asked if she meant harm to anyone in the house. No, came the response. In fact, she was grateful that someone had bought the house and planned to restore it, and indicated that she and her father would help in any way they could!

Erbs started to ask another question but never got the chance. She quickly stood up and walked out the door. Erbs followed seconds later but found nothing. All was quiet in the old house. No footsteps walking away. No doors opening and closing. Only silence . . . and the unnerving experience of having been visited by a lovely young woman who was not of this earth.

Unlike the "classic" ghost or spirit, Erbs's visitor appeared as a solid form. Could it have been a real person? Erbs is convinced it was not. And from all indications it does not seem possible. On both occasions, Marie vanished within seconds of ending her conversations with Erbs. Where could she have gone? Erbs could find no evidence of anyone having entered or left the house despite extensive searches of the entire house after each appearance.

During the second week of September, Paul Ranieri was sitting in the still unfinished front room of the house. It was late in the evening. He had spent the day cleaning and moving furniture. Ranieri was tired and looked forward to the day when the initial repairs were finished and he could finally move in.

As he mulled over the day's work he had the impression of being watched, of knowing in some way that he was not the only one in the room. Turning toward the staircase in an outer hallway, Ranieri saw the figure of a woman emerge from a wall. She glided past him, within inches of where he sat, moved through an archway into a back room, and then seemed to melt into a wall. She said nothing, nor did she look toward him.

Erbs had told Ranieri about his conversations with Marie, of course, and he could see that the figure going past him was remarkably similar in appearance to Erbs's visitor.

Ranieri remained relatively calm as he watched the ghost vanish. "I wasn't really afraid," he recalls. For the first few seconds of her appearance he thought someone had gotten into the house . . . until he realized she was transparent. The wall and some furniture were visible directly behind her!

The entire episode had lasted about fifteen seconds.

Was it a trick of the imagination? The light was dim, coming only from an outside streetlamp directly in front of the house and shining through an uncurtained front window. Was it the way the lights were playing against the dark shapes in the room? Ranieri doesn't think so.

With few exceptions Erbs and Ranieri agree on the woman's physical description: rather young, dark-haired, and dressed in a long dressing gown. The significant difference is that Erbs saw Marie as a solid figure whereas Ranieri's visitor was transparent. But that is not too unusual, as ghosts are reported to change their form during various appearances.

Erbs's next encounter with Marie seemed to indicate that both he and Ranieri had seen the same ghost.

Some ten days after Ranieri's encounter with Marie, Erbs was again alone in the house during the late evening. It was about ten-thirty when Erbs climbed the stairs to his second-floor bedroom. When he reached the top of the staircase and glanced into the room he saw Marie, and this time she was transparent! Momentarily startled, he backed away a few steps and she quickly evaporated.

Why? Erbs thinks his reaction may have

frightened her.

But not for long. A few days later Erbs apparently learned something of Marie's taste in music.

He was in a spare room in his apartment

A window in Marie's home

repairing a broken chair and listening to classical music coming from his record player in the living room. A stack of three records was on the player. The first had only just begun to play when he heard the reject button click . . . once, twice, three times . . . until the unit automatically shut off. Puzzled, he entered the room, but could find nothing wrong with the stereo unit. Erbs had owned the record player for some time and nothing like this had happened before.

Yet every time he started to play classical music the reject button was activated. It never happened with more contemporary, popular music! Was Marie expressing her musical preference? Erbs can find no other explanation.

A few weeks later, Erbs's final conversation with Marie took place—at least until now. It was mid-October. Ranieri and Hicks had moved into the house and were now beginning the tedious process of planning the major renovation of the house.

Interested in any indications of earlier occupants, they started exploring the basement and found fragments of old dishes and jars and other household utensils. Like many older homes, the basement had a dirt floor and was small and cramped by today's standards. It was sectioned off into several rooms with rough hewn doors between the various cubicles.

Eventually, they contacted an archeologist at a local university and asked if he might have an interest in the "dig." Indeed he did! The work stopped until the expert could visit the site.

Shortly thereafter Erbs was again visited in his apartment by Marie. She was concerned about why they weren't working in the basement anymore. After Erbs explained the situation, she asked him to follow her. They walked down to the basement. There she paused and pointed to a wall. He turned to look at the area she motioned toward and when he glanced back in her direction she was gone.

The next day Erbs told Ranieri and Hicks about his visit the night before and his trip to the basement with Marie. After some discussion, the trio decided to examine carefully the wall Marie had pointed to. They discovered that a section of the brick wall was newer than the rest. They knocked out those bricks and started digging in the crawl space beyond. They found pottery shards, pieces of jewelry, and bones. The latter they sent to a museum for analysis. A dog had apparently been buried in that area at one time.

Ranieri speculates that a window or door had been located in that part of the wall and later bricked in. The basement had been the first floor of the house until the early part of this century. As years passed, National Avenue was raised and the yard at the Ranieri home was built up so that the original second floor is now at ground level.

The brick wall they examined is directly under Erbs's apartment, and thus a door or window would have, at one time, looked directly out into the back yard.

The nocturnal visits from Marie are not the only strange occurrences in the house. There is also the smell of roses.

In the early fall, long after the rose bush in a back garden lost its bloom, Ranieri and Hicks would walk into the house after a day at work and be greeted by the aroma of roses. The house had been closed for the day. They knew of no one who had entered or left. Is Marie placing ghostly bouquets around the house to brighten the atmosphere and cheer up the men?

Marie is not the only ghost Ranieri has seen.

Late one night, as Ranieri lay in bed reading, he noticed a pet cat on the other side of the room becoming quite agitated. As he leaned over the edge of the bed to get a better look in that direction, he came eye to eye with an aged bull terrier. He had no such pet in the house! It was not a dream, he says; the lights were on and the cat was clearly cowering under a chair. The dog returned Ranieri's gaze through reddish-tinged eyes and looked decidedly unfriendly. Thinking the door to the room might have been left open, he glanced in that direction but it was securely fastened. When he looked back toward the dog, it had vanished.

No amount of coaxing could get the cat from its hiding place for the rest of the night.

Are the bones found in the basement the earthly remains of that bull terrier?

Ranieri's cat also plays a prominent role in another unusual episode. While working downstairs in the dining room, Ranieri heard the cat growling and mewing from somewhere upstairs. He found her crouching outside an upstairs closet. The door was open but the closet was empty. Ranieri closed the door but the cat stayed outside with its back arched, pacing back and forth. What had the cat seen or sensed? Ranieri saw nothing, but animals often sense psychic forces when humans cannot.

Another household pet, a Siberian Husky, has also been observed playing with something when Ranieri and Hicks can see nothing in the room. Is the dog playing with the ghostly bull terrier or perhaps with Marie herself?

Although he hasn't "seen" Marie, Jeff Hicks has had several unnerving experiences in the house.

Shortly after he moved in, Hicks discovered a door in the basement wedged open. He wanted to get it closed so the Husky couldn't get into an area of the basement not yet cleaned. He tried unsuccessfully to close the door but could move it only a few inches. It was stuck on the uneven floor. About a week later he walked into that area of the basement again, and the door was closed! From that point on he was able to open and close the door halfway before it became stuck again.

Marie had told Erbs that her father could help with the restoration. Did the unseen handyman try to fix the door?

The lights in the basement also seem to have minds of their own. On numerous occasions, often eight to ten times per week, Ranieri or Hicks have opened the basement door to find the lights blazing. No one had been down there. The pair is puzzled since three separate switches must be turned on and that can only be done from the basement.

Is Marie or her father turning on the lights to check on the work progress in the basement?

Hicks's most startling experience occurred in late October as he worked late one night in the basement.

He heard the sound of a dog behind him. Thinking it was the pet Husky, he turned, but nothing was there. The door leading to the upstairs was shut. Yet he heard the distinct sound of metal dog tags and the soft footfalls of a dog's paws on dirt. As he stared at the empty air the sound retreated. Was it the bull terrier?

All three men often feel the "presence" of someone or something, although nothing can be seen. They describe it as a coldness, as if they had suddenly been thrust outside on a wintry day. A draft? Perhaps. But an area that is strangely cold one day is quite warm the next, and the cold spots seem to move about the house.

Is there an explanation for these events? For Marie's visits? Those questions led Ranieri to city records. He has been able to determine that the house was built between 1836 and 1840. It is reputed to be the oldest brick structure in Milwaukee still on its original foundation. At various times it has been a private home, an inn, a restaurant, and, until recently, a rooming house. Such a remarkable history makes determining the basis for a ghost very difficult.

Who is Marie? Ranieri offers two possibilities.

A member of the family that had owned the house for decades told him that a young woman committed suicide in the house during the 1920s. Ranieri has not been able to confirm that account.

A second explanation is that Marie is a young woman who reportedly vanished from the house early in this century. No trace was ever found of her. She apparently walked out of the house one day, leaving her clothes and other personal belongings behind, and was never seen again.

Either story could provide an explanation for Marie's presence.

Ghosts often watch over homes in which they lived and perhaps died a premature death.

And the strange appearance of the bull terrier? Is it Marie's dog? Did she point out its burial place to Donald Erbs that night in the basement?

Erbs and Ranieri saw the ghost on different occasions and in different forms. Although their descriptions vary in some ways, the similarities are striking.

Imagination? Trickery? It doesn't appear likely.

Erbs is still mystified. "For some reason she picked me to talk to. I don't know why. This type of thing has never happened to me before. In fact, before I saw Marie, I didn't believe in ghosts," he maintains.

Does he believe in ghosts now? "Most definitely," he replies.

Do you?

Part VI.
Bay Country Phantoms

THE PHANTOM FUNERAL PROCESSION

The Scots may not be the most superstitious people in the world, but some beliefs they hold tenaciously. One is that the seventh son of a seventh son has precognitive powers, that is, the ability to foretell events. So it was that when Robert Laurie was born in Scotland, news of his birth spread far and wide. As the seventh son of a seventh son, Robert was destined to grow up with the uncanny ability to predict the future.

In 1854, the Lauries emigrated to Wisconsin, settling in Sturgeon Bay. Here young Robert grew into manhood, and his supernatural powers flourished. He told a neighboring family with seven daughters that the eighth child would be a boy. It was. When Robert's brother Alex and another man in the settlement had set forth by boat for Green Bay to get supplies, Robert said they would never return. The boat was never found nor were the men. On a third occasion, Robert assured a neighbor woman that her husband would survive the roiling lake waters after his boat had capsized in a storm. He had "seen" the man clinging to a cabin door that had been torn loose from the craft. Some time later, the door, bearing its human cargo, was washed up on the shore. The seaman was barely conscious, yet alive.

One night when Robert Laurie was in his sixties, he had a dream so vivid that in the morning he was impelled to tell it to his wife. He told her there would soon be a large funeral in Door County and that people would come great distances by land and by water to attend. He described the shining horses pulling magnificent carriages; he named the minister and number of mourners. The only thing he did not know was the name of the deceased.

A month later, the funeral was held. People came from near and far, and all the details of the service were exactly as Robert had foreseen them. But, among the mourners there was one whose heart was heaviest with sorrow—the dreamer's widow, Catherine.

THE GRAY LADY

Sixty-odd years ago Ruth Baker and her family lived on the old Kopelkie farm, about ten miles west of Shawano. While eating dinner one evening, Ruth noticed a woman walking in the hallway beyond an open door. She jumped up and ran to the cellar where her mother was getting butter from the crock. "Mommy," she cried, "I just saw a fairy! She was a nurse. And she wore a gray-and-white-striped dress."

Ruth, her mother, her younger brother, and an uncle searched the hall and the upstairs rooms but found no sign of the mysterious lady.

Later, Ruth's grandmother recalled that a previous occupant had also seen an apparition. It was thought that the ghost had some connection with a man who had been ill and died in the isolated farmhouse.

A SUMMONS FROM THE GRAVE

In 1935, Esther Johnson* and her husband, of Manitowoc, were renting the upstairs apartment in a private home, a small but quiet place that met their needs.

The bedroom had two doors diagonally across from each other, leaving just enough room for the bed in the corner. The door near the foot of the bed, leading to a central hall, was not used. It was kept closed and locked; a wardrobe stood against it on one side and a china closet on the other. The second door, near the head of the bed, opened into a rear room that also had another door leading into the hall at the place where the stairway led down to the first floor.

One night after the couple had retired, Esther saw the apparition of a tall woman, wearing a long gray dress and matching sweater, emerging from the wardrobe. The ghost walked with folded arms and bowed head; she moved slowly around the bed and never looked at its occupants. Esther nudged her husband, who, she recalls, "couldn't have been more than thirty inches from her as she passed." He said, "Can't Mrs. Anderson* walk in her own house if she wants to?"

The apparition vanished through the door into the rear room, and the tenants, not in the least frightened, fell promptly asleep.

Not until morning did the Johnsons learn that their landlord, Mr. Anderson,* had died in his first-floor apartment. Only his wife had known the moment of death and had come for him.

She had been dead for nineteen years.

HOUSE OF CHIMES

The George Websters moved into an old house in Green Bay in 1968. Everything went well at first. Then, the kitchen screen door, equipped with a tight spring, began opening and slamming shut with no one near it and no wind blowing. George recalls that on one occasion the slamming was preceded by "a loud scraping, swirling noise." He had been standing only twenty feet from the door. He rushed outside to investigate but found nothing that could account for the noise or the movement of the door.

On July 20, 1976, George was home alone doing paperwork in connection with his job as district supervisor for a Chicago-based corporation. He had just started for the back bedroom when he heard the now-familiar slam. Looking toward the door, he saw the apparition of a man approaching—a black-clothed specter who seemed to float rather than walk. It came straight toward him and George flattened himself against a wall to let it pass. Then the ghost, as if sensing a head-on collision, veered to the right and passed within two feet of the homeowner. It turned its head to stare at him, entered a bedroom, and vanished. George estimates that the episode took place in about ten seconds.

Five days later the family left on a vacation trip. The house was locked up and empty, or so they thought. At nine o'clock that night the neighbors, who were taking in Websters' mail, saw the kitchen lights go on and dark apparitions move back and forth in the room.

One day in August, Mrs. Webster watched two white-clad ghosts disappear into the master bedroom that is just off the kitchen.

Some time later, the family began hearing "scraping and screeching noises in between the walls." Playful mice? Hardly. George says, "These noises would then turn into chimes and bell-like noises." Lights also were being turned on and off by unseen forces both day and night, and neighbors often called the Websters to find out why they had left their basement lights on all night.

On September 3, 1977, the family moved. The old house remained vacant for three months before it sold and, although the electricity was shut off, neighbors reported that the lights continued to go on intermittently during that entire time. George then talked with the former owner of the place, who said he had never witnessed any strange phenomena during his stay in the house.

What does George make of these bizarre manifestations? He has no explanation; he says only that he believes his experiences are "most unusual."

Selected Bibliography

BOOKS

Chapin, Earl. *Tales of Wisconsin.* Compiled and edited by Wayne Wolfe. River Falls: University of Wisconsin-River Falls Press, 1973.

Cole, Harry E. *Stagecoach and Tavern Tales of the Old Northwest.* Cleveland: Arthur H. Clarke, 1930.

Conard, Howard Louis, ed. *History of Milwaukee: From Its First Settlement to the Year 1895.* Vol. 1. Chicago and New York: American Biographical Publishing Co., n.d.

Gard, Robert, and Sorden, L.G. *Wisconsin Lore.* New York: Duell, Sloan, and Pearce, 1962.

Gilman, Rhoda R. *Historic Chequamegon.* 1971.

Holzhueter, John O. *Madeline Island and the Chequamegon Region.* Madison: State Historical Society of Wisconsin, 1974.

Lewis, Jeanie. *Ridgeway Host to the Ghost.* Dodgeville: Dodgeville Chronicle, 1975.

Napoli, James. *The Coasts of Wisconsin.* Madison: University of Wisconsin Sea Grant College Program, March 1975.

Owen, A. R. G. *Can We Explain the Poltergeists.* Chicago: Regnery, 1954.

Strait, William E. *Camp Fires at La Pointe: An Historical Journey through the Centuries in La Pointe.* n.d.

Stresau, Marion. *Tomorrows Unlimited.* Boston: Branden Press, 1973.

Thurston, Herbert, S. J. *Ghosts and Poltergeists.* Chicago: Regnery, 1954.

Williams, Mentor L., ed. *Schoolcraft's Indian Legends.* Westport, Conn.: Greenwood Press, 1956.

PERIODICALS

Bednarek, Jim. "The Legend of Mary Buth." *Germantown Press,* September 1, 1977.

Burnett County Sentinel, October 4, 1889.

Daily Milwaukee News, August 9, 1874.

Doehlert, Betsy. "Do Ghosts Walk Aboretum Glades?" *Capital Times* (Madison), October 31, 1977.

Dorschner, Cheri. "Paine Art Center: History Haunts Paine's Past." *Oshkosh Advance-Titan* (University of Wisconsin-Oshkosh), October 13, 1977

Dunn County News, September 13, 1873; October 25, 1873; November 8, 1873.

Durand Weekly Times, September 12, 1873; September 26, 1873, October 3, 1873.

Franklin, Dixie. "New Light Shed on Odd Light." *Milwaukee Journal,* August 6, 1978.

"The Ghost Hunter's Handiguide." *Wisconsin Week-End,* October 1978.

Heinen, Thomas. "Tragedy Stalks a Farmhouse." *Milwaukee Journal,* October 25, 1977.

Hudson Star and Times, December 8, 1869.

Lenz, Elmer, "Have You Seen the Light?" *Milwaukee Badge,* July 1977.

Madison Daily Democrat, December 5, 1873.

Miller, Willis. Editor's Column. *Hudson Star-Observer,* September 14, 1944.

Milwaukee News, October 16, 1973.

Milwaukee Sentinel, August 11, 1875; September 26, 1878; February 14, 1897.

Mt. Horeb Times, March 18, 1909; March 25, 1909; April 1, 1909; April 8, 1909; April 15, 1909; April 11, 1909.

Orton, Charles, W. "The Haunting." *Wisconsin Trails,* Autumn 1976.

Orum, Alma. "Octagon House Has Spirit, But No Ghost." *Milwaukee Sentinel,* January 3, 1960.

Oshkosh Weekly Times, November 25, 1873; December 3, 1873.

Peterson, Gary. "Time Plays Tricks with Memory of 1909 Mt. Horeb Poltergeist." *Capital Times* (Madison), October 26, 1978.

Pett, Mrs. W. F. "A Forgotten Village." *Wisconsin Magazine of History.* September 1928.

Reuschlein, Harrison. "Mischief on the High Hill Where Jenny Lies Buried." *Wisconsin Week-End,* December 7, 1977.

River Falls Journal, September 23, 1873; October 31, 1873; December 12, 1873.

Rogo, D. Scott. "More about the Poltergeist: The Power Behind Teenage Tantrums." *Human Behavior,* May 1978.

Waukesha Freeman, July 18, 1918; July 25, 1918.

Wisconsin State Journal (Madison), August 11, 1874; March 30, 1909; April 2, 1909.

Unpublished Works

Madison, Wisconsin. State Historical Society of Wisconsin. Charles E. Brown Papers. Wisconsin Mss. HB. Boxes 7 and 9.

Nielsen, A. J. "He Came with the House." May 9, 1977.

Orton, Charles W. "Ridgeway Ghost Tales."

Van Dyke, Madge Patterson. "The Story of Kilbourn and Its Vicinity." Bachelor's thesis, University of Wisconsin, 1916.

Beth Scott & Michael Norman

Beth Scott has been a free-lance writer for twenty-five years, with stories, articles and light verse appearing in publications in this country and abroad.

She was formerly an editor's assistant in a technical publishing house, a newspaper columnist and a teacher of creative writing in an adult education program.

A native of Ardmore, Pennsylvania, Mrs. Scott holds the B.A. degree in English from the University of Pennsylvania. She did graduate work at Kansas State University and Oregon State University, where she studied writing with Bernard Malamud. Since 1961, she and her husband have lived in River Falls. They have three grown children.

Michael Norman has taught journalism at the University of Wisconsin-River Falls since 1973.

Norman, 33, has worked as a newspaper sports writer, radio news director, high school teacher, gardener and factory worker. He is a native of southern Illinois but attended high school in suburban Chicago. He holds the M.S. degree in journalism from Northern Illinois University. He is married and the father of one son.